Success Habits of Christian Millionaires

Updated & Expanded Edition

How to change your life and make more money

with time-tested strategies used by

Christian millionaires (and billionaires)

Michael Holmes

ISBN-13: 978-1793143983

ISBN-10: 1793143986

Foreword to the Expanded Edition

Why There's Now a Story in This Book

When this book first went out into the world, it was teaching — principle after principle, habit after habit, the secrets that took me from months behind on rent to a multi six-figure earner. Hundreds of you read it. Many of you wrote to me. And a pattern showed up in what you said.

You understood the habits. You just couldn't always *see* them.

You knew you were supposed to seek God first — but what does that look like on a Tuesday when the rent's due? You know gratitude unlocks increase — but how does a man actually live that when his father just died and his faith is hanging by a thread? The principle was clear. The picture was missing.

So I gave you a picture.

In the second half of this book you'll meet DeMarcus. He's a young man who loves God and keeps failing Him — lust in the evening, guilt in the morning, the war Paul described in Romans 7 playing out in one ordinary life. He's broke. He's stuck. And over the chapters ahead, one habit at a time, you'll watch him climb. Everything you learn in Book One, you'll watch him live in Book Two.

I didn't invent this method. I borrowed it from the best Teacher who ever lived.

> *"All these things spake Jesus unto the multitude in parables; and without a parable spake he not unto them." (Matthew 13:34 KJV)*

Think about that. The Son of God could have handed us a clean list of rules. Instead He told stories — a sower, a son who ran off and came home, a man who buried his talent in the ground. Why? Because a truth you're *told* sits in your head. A truth you *watch happen* drops into your heart. The parable does what the lecture can't: it makes you *feel* the thing before you're asked to do it.

That's what DeMarcus is. He's the parable for these habits. He's the secrets with skin on.

Now, one honest word. The story follows a young man — his struggles, his fight, his rise. But hear me: **the principles in this book have no gender.** They are immutable, consequential, and universal. They worked for Drenda Keesee on her knees at midnight and for the twin brothers flipping a phone book; they'll work for you, woman or man, the same way gravity works for everyone who steps off a ledge. I wrote DeMarcus as one specific man for the same reason Jesus wrote one specific prodigal son — truth cuts deepest when it bleeds through a single life. Walk with him. The lesson is yours no matter who you are.

So here's how to read what's coming. Book One sets your mind and gives you the habits. Book Two lets you watch a man live them out. Read them in order. Let the teaching instruct you, and let the story convict you.

You came here because you love God and you want more — more freedom, more provision, more of the abundant life He actually promised. Good. You're in the right place.

Turn the page. Let's set your mind. Then let's go meet DeMarcus.

Table of Contents

BOOK ONE

Success Habits of Christian Millionaires

The Teaching

Introduction

It Is Possible to Love God, Do His Work, AND Be Affluent

> *"He replied, 'You are permitted to understand the secret of the Kingdom of God. But I use parables for everything I say to outsiders.'"* (Mark 4:11 NLT)*

Of the millions of millionaires in the world, the majority identify as Christian. Far more than any other group. In other words:

It IS possible to love God, do His work, AND be affluent.

So what are the "secrets" that caused *these* believers to build wealth while other believers stay stuck in poverty? That was the question I was determined to answer. What were the secrets that changed their lives?

When Do Won Chang and his wife Jin Sook arrived on U.S. soil, they were desperate for those secrets. They had escaped South Korea and were looking for a way up. For a while they struggled — multiple jobs, not enough income, one short-lived position after another. Then everything changed when they were shown a secret. Other secrets followed, and in time the Changs built Forever 21 into a multi-billion-dollar fashion empire. (Keep their name in mind. Their story has a second half most people don't know — and we'll get to it, because it teaches as much as the rise did.)

Steven K. Scott was hunting for these secrets too. He was a below-average earner who flunked out of *nine* jobs in his first six years after college. Then a friend prayed for him, God dropped a secret into that friend's heart, and armed with it Scott went on to build a dozen companies and over a billion dollars in sales.

Gary Keesee needed a secret badly. He and his wife were in debt up to their eyeballs — finance-company loans at 28% interest, back taxes, money owed to relatives, judgments and liens. He couldn't provide the basics for his family. Then, out of money and out of options, he cried out to God — and in mercy, God gave him a secret. Over time he and his wife got completely out of debt, built companies that produced millions, and now teach others what they learned.

I'd love to tell you my life wasn't like those stories. I'd be lying. Not long ago my life was in shambles:

- I was months behind on rent.
- My finances were a disaster.
- A friend suggested I look into welfare.

I had no hope. That was until God tossed me a glimpse of a secret. And He was wise about it — He never forced it on me. He waited until I'd exhausted all *my* options and was at the end of my rope. Then, instead of pointing a condemning finger, He gave me His compassionate hand and pulled me up out of the mess I'd made. He showed me a secret. And that secret — with others like it — led me from debt and discouragement to becoming a six-figure earner.

So What Are These "Secrets"?

> *"The secret of the LORD is with them that fear him; and he will shew them his covenant."* (Psalm 25:14 KJV)*

That word **"secret"** is the Hebrew word **"sod."** It means a *session*, a *fixed counsel or design*, a *couch* — and the confidential talk of those sitting on it. These secrets are fixed designs God has in place, revealed in intimate communion with those He loves and who love Him. They are His highest plans for each person — for occupation, for family, for ministry, and yes, for money and abundance.

> *"'For I know the plans I have for you,' declares the LORD, 'plans to prosper you and not to harm you, plans to give you hope and a future.'"* (Jeremiah 29:11 NIV)*

Are these secrets *really* secret? No. They were hidden *for* the benefit of those who would search them out.

> *"It is the glory of God to conceal a thing: but the honour of kings is to search out a matter."* (Proverbs 25:2 KJV)*

And these secrets — like God's laws — have three characteristics:

1. **They are immutable.** They don't change. They're constant and consistent, and because of that you can rely on a consistent outcome.
2. **They are consequential.** Followed, they bring consistent rewards. Disobeyed, they bring equally consistent consequences.
3. **They are universal.** They work for anyone. They are neither for us nor against us — they work *with* us as we work with them.

One last thing. What made these Christian millionaires (and billionaires) so successful is that they made these secrets **habitual.** They practiced them. They perfected them. So the real secret is this: they learned the secrets and then turned them into *habits* — and those habits, repeated over and over, changed their lives.

Once you learn them, it's up to you to do the same.

> *"Beloved, I wish above all things that thou mayest prosper and be in health, even as thy soul prospereth."* (3 John 2 KJV)*

That word **"prosper"** is the Greek word **"euodoo"** — "a good road," "a good journey." That's my prayer for you: a good and prosperous journey, into a new realm of abundance where your purpose, your passion, and His plan intersect.

I'll see you on the other side.

PART ONE – THE FOUNDATION

Mindset Before Method

✦ ✦ ✦

The Diligent Mind

Foundation Opener

Wealth is built with two hands.

In one hand is the **skill set** — the doing. The working, the managing, the selling, the building. This book is full of it. You'll watch a man save a fortune by removing one drop of solder. You'll watch a broke idealist outlast a corrupt government. You'll watch twins turn a stack of pallets into an empire.

But there's a second hand. And it moves first.

In the other hand is the **mindset** — the thinking. Most people get this backwards. They believe the work produces the wealth and the mindset is a nice-to-have, a little positivity sprinkled on top.

It's the other way around.

> *"The thoughts of the diligent tend only to plenteousness; but of every one that is hasty only to want."* (Proverbs 21:5 KJV)*

Read that slowly. Before there is plenty, there are **thoughts**. The diligent don't stumble into abundance — their *thinking* points there first. The mind leans toward plenty, and the hands follow.

Solomon says it even sharper:

> *"For as he thinketh in his heart, so is he."* (Proverbs 23:7 KJV)*

So is he. Not "so he hopes." Not "so he pretends." So he *is*. What you rehearse in private, you eventually live in public.

Now — be careful, because there's a counterfeit close by. The counterfeit says: *picture the money and the money will appear.*

Sit still, visualize the car, and the universe mails it to you. That's not what Scripture teaches, and it's not what built a single fortune in this book.

Look at the verse again. The diligent *think* toward plenty — and *because* they think that way, they *become diligent.* The thought doesn't replace the work. **The thought produces the work.** An abundant mind can't sit still. It sees past its circumstances, refuses "want" as the final word, and that refusal puts the hands in motion. Thought, then diligence, then harvest. In that order. Every time.

That's the difference between this book and the shelf full of "manifest your millions" books next to it. We're not asking you to wish. We're telling you the way you think will decide how hard, how smart, and how long you work — and God blesses the labor your mindset sets in motion.

> *"If you will only let me help you, if you will only obey, then I will make you rich!"* (Isaiah 1:19 TLB)*

He helps. You obey. Both hands move.

Here's the order of this book, and it's deliberate:

Part One — The Foundation. Before we touch a single money-making tactic, we set the mind. You'll learn to seek God first, to live in gratitude — the rule that opens the floodgates of increase — to see a vision bigger than your bank account, and to find the one lane where you were built to win. Get this wrong and no amount of hustle will save you. Get it right and the rest has somewhere to land.

Part Two — The Build. Now the hands. Giving, going the extra mile, out-working the room, taking holy risks, managing every dollar, and refusing to quit. This is where the money gets made.

Part Three — The Legacy. Because wealth was never the finish line. Wealth in good hands does great things — it solves problems at scale, and it outlives the one who built it. We end where every Christian millionaire's story is meant to end: not with what you kept, but with what you left.

You were not handed an abundant God and a poverty mind by accident. The mind is yours to renew — *"be ye transformed by the renewing of your mind"* (Romans 12:2). That renewal starts on the next page.

Let's set your mind. Then let's build.

✦ ✦ ✦

Habit 1

The Habit of Seeking God First

After Do Won and Jin Sook Chang arrived on U.S. soil, they went straight to work. Do Won landed on a Saturday and didn't waste a day — he scoured the classifieds, landed an interview, and by Monday he was prepping meals in a coffee shop for $3 an hour. To stretch their income he pumped gas and started an office-cleaning business; Jin Sook worked as a hairdresser.

It still wasn't enough.

While pumping gas, Do Won noticed something: the fashion retailers drove the nice cars. So he got a job at a clothing store. And around the same time, Jin Sook went up to a mountain to pray. She wanted answers about their finances. On that mountain, she became convinced God told her they should open a store — and that it would be successful.

She came home and told her husband what she'd heard. And the idea for Forever 21 was born. In their first year they did $700,000 in sales. Within a generation it was a global, multi-billion-dollar company.

But ask yourself: what if they'd never sought God? What if they'd said, "We can figure this out on our own"? Maybe they'd have found *some* success. But imagine the time they saved by seeking God first. Even at their peak, the family said their biggest business ideas came out of early-morning prayer.

Christian Millionaires Seek God First

One of the great strengths of Christian entrepreneurs is their ability to hear and obey the voice of God. Yes, they work hard. Yes, they're diligent strategists and team builders. But their ability to obey God's promptings is what sets them apart.

When twin brothers Jason and David Benham went into real estate, they had no niche. Rather than try to "figure it out," they hit their knees and committed to pray for fourteen straight days for direction. On the fourteenth day, a bank called — they'd been flipping through the phone book — and asked if the Benhams would sell a foreclosed property. That phone call was the beginning of more than 23,000 foreclosed homes sold over the next decade.

Remember Gary and Drenda Keesee and their mountain of debt? One night Drenda was desperate. It made no sense — they loved the Lord but were drowning. She decided she would not go to bed until God explained what was happening and how to fix it. She prayed, searched the Scriptures, and landed in the book of Haggai:

> *"You have sown much, and bring in little... and he who earns wages, earns wages to put into a bag with holes... 'Consider your ways!'"* (Haggai 1:6–7 NKJV)*

The revelation hit her: they had never sought God for *His* plan. They'd made their own plans and asked God to bless them. (Have you ever done that?) After that, God gave them *His* plan — to start a business helping people get out of debt. She woke Gary up to tell him. His response? "Well, if that's true, I wish He'd tell me how to get out of debt first." Then he rolled over and went back to sleep. (God dealt with him later — and Gary had to apologize.)

A Modern Witness: David Steward

Consider David Steward. He grew up poor in Missouri, one of eight children, and faced obstacle after obstacle in his early career. He started a technology company out of near-nothing and built it into World Wide Technology — today one of the largest such firms in the country, with revenues in the billions, making Steward one of the wealthiest Black businessmen in America.

And he says it plainly: he attributes his success to faith and perseverance, leading his company on biblical principles of integrity, servant leadership, and generosity. He didn't seek fortune first. He sought God first — and built a culture around it.

The Lesson: God wants you to succeed more than you could possibly realize. So seek His plan, His will, His direction — *before* you draw up your own and ask Him to rubber-stamp it. He'll lead you in the way you're supposed to go.

✦ ✦ ✦

Habit 2

The Habit of Gratitude

The habit is simple: before you can have more, you must be grateful for what you have now. The Bible is very clear: *"In every thing give thanks: for this is the will of God in Christ Jesus concerning you."* (1 Thessalonians 5:18 KJV)

Let me show you why with a story.

Imagine you have two sons whom you love very much. You provide for them, care for them, give everything you have. Yet they respond to you in totally different ways.

Your first son is a cynic. Logical to a fault, doesn't trust you much, says hurtful things. You serve him breakfast and he says: *"Eggs again? Didn't we have eggs yesterday? We never have real food. If I can't trust you with breakfast, how can I trust you with lunch? And what about dinner — do you even love me?"*

You probably had to restrain yourself reading that.

Then there's your other son. Not as "logical." He just believes you love him, will keep loving him, and will always take care of him. Same breakfast, different response: *"Wow — thank you for this, it looks great. And thank you for all the times you've fed me. You've been good to me my whole life. I have a roof, clothes, a bed, everything I need. Thank you."*

Now tell me honestly: **which son are you more willing to bless a little more?**

Selah.

Christian Millionaires Live in Thanksgiving

God hates an ungrateful spirit. I don't say that lightly — He says it. Of those who turned from Him, Paul writes that *"although they knew God, they neither glorified him as God, neither were thankful... and their foolish heart was darkened."* (Romans 1:21)

Catch the order. Ingratitude came first. The darkened, broke, futile thinking came *after*. The unthankful heart is the soil bad thinking grows in. And the reverse is just as true — a thankful heart is the soil increase grows in.

Here's something most people never notice. The word **"affluence"** comes from the Latin **affluere** — "to flow to." To be affluent is to have abundance *flow* into your life. And what do we call money? **Currency** — same root as *current*, something that flows.

Gratitude opens the floodgates.

> *True wealth ALWAYS begins with a wealthy state of mind. Gratitude is what cultivates that mind. Increase begins the moment you are grateful for what you already have.*

This is the mindset half of wealth — and it comes first.

"God Gave Me My Money"

Are you familiar with John D. Rockefeller? He was the richest Christian who ever lived. Don't let the rumors fool you. But watch his *heart* for a moment, because the man was thankful to his bones. He never wavered on where his fortune came from — he said, plainly: **"God gave me my money."** A settled, grateful certainty that everything he had was a gift to be stewarded. Rockefeller didn't grumble his way to a fortune. He gave thanks on his way there.

And this law is so woven into how abundance moves that even the secular world keeps tripping over it. Sir John Templeton, who built one of the great investment fortunes of the twentieth century and managed billions, taught that an attitude of gratitude is itself what opens the door to blessing — to wake each morning expecting good and giving thanks for life itself. He wasn't preaching a sermon. He was reporting what he'd observed building wealth for forty years. **Wall Street simply found what Scripture stated first.**

Thanksgiving Is a Sign of Faith

Now it goes deeper than manners.

It's one thing to thank someone *after* they give you something. It's another to thank them *before*. The first is an act of **gratitude.** The second is an act of **faith.**

> *"Now faith is the substance of things hoped for, the evidence of things not seen."* (Hebrews 11:1 KJV)*

The Amplified calls faith the *title deed* of things hoped for — ownership on paper before you ever hold the thing. If I gave you my car keys and said it was yours, it would mean nothing in court, because the title deed is still in my name. Faith *is* the title deed. So when Paul says, *"by prayer and supplication with thanksgiving let your requests be made known unto God"* (Philippians 4:6), he means: give thanks for what you've asked *before it shows up*. That's not pretending. That's faith laying hold of the deed.

Watch how Jesus did it. In one instance, He had five loaves, two fish, and five thousand men plus women and children to feed. It wasn't **enough.** But before He broke a single loaf, He gave thanks — and what was not enough became more than enough. The thanksgiving came *before* the multiplication. It always does.

And that — to be clear — is the difference between this and the empty "manifest your millions" noise. We're not telling you to picture money into existence. We're telling you to be so grateful, and so sure of a good Father, that you thank Him in advance and then *go to work* with that confidence. Thanksgiving, then faith, then diligent hands, then harvest.

Thanksgiving Is a Lifestyle

This was never meant to be a holiday in November. It's the mark of a mature person — *"rooted and built up in him...*

abounding therein with thanksgiving" (Colossians 2:7 KJV). Let your living *spill over* into thanks. On the good days and the lean ones. The grateful heart doesn't wait for a reason — it *is* the reason increase comes looking.

The Lesson — and Your Assignment:

- **Take inventory.** Before you ask for more, thank Him — out loud, specifically — for what's already in your hands.
- **Thank Him in advance.** Pick the thing you're believing for and start thanking Him for it now, as faith — then move your feet toward it.
- **Kill the murmuring.** For one week, refuse to complain. Catch every ungrateful word and replace it with thanks.
- **Make it a lifestyle, not an event.**

The cynical son got the same breakfast as the grateful one. But only one of them was getting a bigger lunch. Be the grateful son.

✦ ✦ ✦

Habit 3

The Habit of the Big Vision

Steven K. Scott was the embodiment of a mess. Saved, loved the Lord — and flunked out of nine jobs after college. With a young family to support, he was desperate. After he lost job number six, he went to his best friend, Gary Smalley, and said: "I don't understand — no matter how hard I work, I just can't succeed."

Smalley said he'd pray about it. The next morning he came back with a challenge: read one chapter of Proverbs every day for two years, write down the insights, and apply them to your work.

Scott had nothing to lose. He did it.

On job number nine, he built a TV marketing campaign that doubled the company's sales in four months. At 27 his boss offered to double his salary, make him VP of marketing, and hand him a company car. Instead, Scott resigned to start his own marketing company with a partner and $5,000. Within nine months, sales hit nearly *one million dollars a week.*

What changed? Scott learned the secret of **vision-mapping.** In his words, in his failed jobs he never had a clear, precise picture of what he wanted to achieve — so they fizzled. But on his tenth job he had a detailed roadmap: where he was, where he was going, the exact steps to get there.

> *"Where there is no vision, the people perish."* (Proverbs 29:18 KJV)*

Most people have *no* vision. Or if they do it's a vague and fuzzy one ("be more successful, get richer, slim down"). That's not a vision. A true vision is a detailed roadmap. God Himself said:

> *"Write this. Write what you see. Write it out in big block letters so that it can be read on the run. This vision-message is a witness pointing to what's coming. It aches for the*

> *coming—it can hardly wait! And it doesn't lie. If it seems slow in coming, wait. It's on its way. It will come right on time." Habakkuk 2:2-3 (The Message)*

It has to be specific, measurable, and written for it to become possible.

Don't Just Be S.M.A.R.T. — Shoot for the Moon

When people speak about goal-setting they love the S.M.A.R.T. formula — Specific, Measurable, Achievable, **Realistic**, Time-bound. The problem is "realistic." Realistic goals don't change the world or produce super-achievers. It's when we set *impossible* goals that we maximize our potential. Why? Because Christian millionaires never forget the **God factor.** They figured out early that they're in partnership with a God bigger than any obstacle, who can do more than they could ask or think.

This is a recurring pattern of God — He gives the grand vision *first*:

- Abraham saw countless descendants while still childless.
- Joseph saw his future before he ever lived it.
- Rockefeller, as a young bookkeeper, was always "getting ready for something big."

So — do you have a grand vision? Is it bigger than your current capabilities? Does it cost more than you have? Is it further than where you are? **Good.** That means you're on the right path.

The Power of Wise Counsel

Notice something easy to miss in Scott's story: the breakthrough didn't start with Scott. It started with **Gary Smalley** — a wise friend who prayed and handed him the Proverbs challenge. Scott's million-dollar vision was *seeded by counsel.*

> *"Where no counsel is, the people fall: but in the multitude of counsellors there is safety."* (Proverbs 11:14 KJV)*

"Plans fail for lack of counsel, but with many advisers they succeed." (Proverbs 15:22 NIV)*

Wealthy people are not lone geniuses. They build boards, mentors, masterminds, and trusted advisers around their vision. A vision held alone is fragile. A vision surrounded by godly counsel is *armored.* Don't just dream big — dream big *in company.*

Your assignment:

- **Get in the Presence of God and ask Him about your goals.**
- **Write them down** — no matter how far-fetched. Put *dates* on the impossible ones.
- **Put them where you'll see them daily** — mirror, vision board, steering wheel.
- **Rewrite them often.** There's a benefit to re-writing: it etches the vision into your mind and steers your life toward it.
- **Surround the vision with counsel.** Find your Gary Smalley.

✦ ✦ ✦

Habit 4

The Habit of Purpose

In 2009, Simon Sinek gave a TED Talk that became one of the most-watched ever. The core idea: people don't care *what* you do, they care *why* you do it. Ordinary leaders start with what, then how, then why. World-changers start with **why** – they speak from a deeper meaning, and they accomplish more because of it.

What makes Christian millionaires so powerful is their commitment to their individual purpose. They understand who they are – and who they are *not*.

Like the Apostle Paul. He wasn't a "Christian millionaire," but he was effective because he understood his purpose, embraced it, and never strayed from it. He understood his **"sphere."**

> *"We... will not boast beyond measure, but within the limits of the sphere which God appointed us... not to boast in another man's sphere."* (2 Corinthians 10:13–16 NKJV)*

That word **"sphere"** is the Greek **"kanon"** – "a boundary or place of activity." When we truly understand our purpose, we understand our place of activity. We find our greatest fruitfulness in our sphere. Trouble begins when we stray out of it.

David Green Learned It the Hard Way

David Green is the founder of Hobby Lobby, today a retail giant with revenues topping seven billion dollars and more than 900 stores. He's known for generosity and stewardship – for sticking to his "why" and glorifying God in business. But in the 1980s, he got off track.

During the oil boom, cash was everywhere, and you could sell almost anything for a profit. Green admits they drifted out of their craft-store sweet spot – selling expensive luggage, grandfather clocks, ceiling fans, gourmet food, even miniature brass oil rigs. The incoming cash was covering the mistakes. Then came the bust of 1985. Money dried up. By year's end he'd lost nearly a million dollars. The bank threatened to call his note. Suppliers cut him off.

Every day, he says, he crawled under his desk and cried out to God. And in time the direction came: *get back to your core business; tighten your belt everywhere.* He found a new lender, renegotiated with suppliers, and returned to what he knew best. By the end of 1986 he was out of the red and profitable again.

The answer was simple: **go back to your sphere.**

The Other Half of the Forever 21 Story

In the introduction I told you Do Won and Jin Sook Chang built Forever 21 into a multi-billion-dollar empire after seeking God. That's true. But there's a second half, and it's the most important lesson in this chapter.

Forever 21 grew explosively — and kept growing, into enormous multi-level stores in premium malls, into market after market, far beyond the lean, trend-fast formula that built it. They expanded out past their sphere. When the retail world shifted — when nimble online competitors undercut them and mall traffic dried up — that overextended footprint became an anchor. The company filed for bankruptcy in 2019, restructured, and then in 2025 filed a *second* time and liquidated. Its U.S. stores closed for good.

Let that land. The *same* couple, the *same* gift, the *same* God who gave Jin Sook a vision on a mountain. The rise came from seeking God and staying in their lane. The fall came, in large part, from straying out of it — from chasing scale beyond the boundary of what they did best.

Wealth that wanders out of its sphere is wealth at risk. The lesson isn't "don't grow." It's *growing inside your calling.*

The Lesson: Stay in Your Lane

There is a "sweet spot" you have, whether you know it yet or not. If you know it: stay there, be fruitful there, maximize potential there. If you *don't* know it: go to God. He knows your strengths better than you do — He made you. Ignore the voices telling you to chase someone else's lane. Your success is in your sphere, not somebody else's.

PART TWO — THE BUILD

The Money-Making Habits

✦ ✦ ✦

Habit 5

The Habit of Giving

Before John D. Rockefeller became one of the richest men in American history — before his personal wealth equaled a stunning share of the entire U.S. economy, before his philanthropy ran into the hundreds of millions — he learned to give as a boy. With his first job at sixteen, he gave 6% of his earnings to charity. By twenty, his giving exceeded 10% of his income, much of it to his church.

A devout Christian, Rockefeller believed his success was divinely inspired, and he believed he'd been entrusted with wealth *because* he would steward and return it. That belief didn't begin when he was a tycoon. It began when he had low pay, no name, and big dreams.

Christian Millionaires Practice the Strategy of Giving

In our culture, tithing is treated as a hoax or a joke. In Jewish culture it's treated as an ancient formula for becoming wealthy. The Talmud says, *"Tithe so that you will become rich"* (Taanit 9a). Tithing is a **partnership**: the giver partners with God in helping the world, and God partners with the giver in business affairs.

When the Bible speaks of the tithe it uses the Hebrew word **"maascr."** And here's the beauty of Hebrew — it's a language of root words.

Take the first letter, **mem (מ)**, off of *maaser*, and you're left with **"aser"** — which means **rich.** Another way to read it: *the one who tithes becomes rich.*

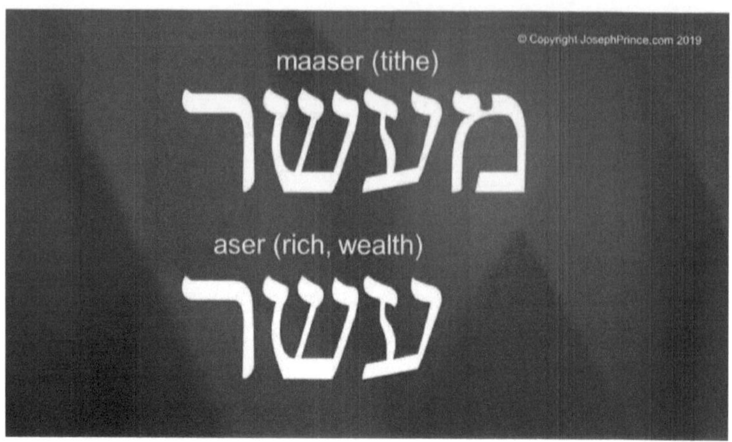

Whoa.

Enter **Chantel Ray.** Before she was a multi-million-dollar real estate entrepreneur, she was a youth pastor making $9 an hour and living on credit cards — $10,000 in debt, cards maxed. Then she heard about tithing. Like most of us, she said, "Yeah, right — maybe when I make some money." But after months of things getting worse, she took the leap. Her first tithe check was $30. The next day she got a refund check for $300. She kept tithing — a relative felt led to pay off her debt. She kept tithing — within months, a better job. She kept tithing, and increased it — a new career in real estate, top salesperson, then her own firm.

My Own "Tithing Experiment"

My finances were in shambles, as I told you. While praying, I opened to Malachi:

> *"Bring all the tithes into the storehouse... 'I will pour out a blessing so great you won't have enough room to take it in! Try it! Put me to the test!'"* (Malachi 3:10 NLT)*

My response: *"Sooooo... let me get this straight. I have NO money, and You want me to give money away?"* Silence. "Hellooo?" More silence. The page just said: *Try it! Put Me to the test.*

I'd love to tell you I went all-in immediately. The truth? I shut the Bible and tried to figure out something else. It took a couple of months before I finally tried this "tithing experiment." And my life was never the same. I became a six-figure earner, and I learned to manage money so well I got out of debt in short order.

These aren't isolated stories. A landmark study of more than 5,000 tithers and non-tithers found tithers were consistently better off financially — more likely to be debt-free, less likely to be buried in credit-card debt, more likely to have assets and a will. The author noted that people who follow biblical giving principles tend to be wiser and more careful with money; generosity leads to financial freedom, while withholding tends to lead toward bondage.

The Modern Master of This Habit: Alan Barnhart

If you want to see this principle running at full power in our lifetime, look at Alan Barnhart. When he and his brother Eric took over the family crane-and-rigging business, Alan spent two years studying what the Bible says about money — and what he found scared him. So they did something almost unheard of: they *capped their own salaries*, deciding that if the business succeeded, they wouldn't see it as a license to inflate their lifestyle.

The business *did* succeed — Barnhart Crane & Rigging grew into a company doing more than $400 million in revenue. And the brothers gave. The first year they gave away $50,000 — more than Alan's salary. Then $150,000. Then a million a year. Then a million a *month*. Eventually they gave away the *entire company* into a charitable trust, and today they channel something like twenty million dollars a year into ministry — while insisting **THEY'VE** been the *beneficiaries*.

"God is the owner; you are the steward." That's how Barnhart frames it. He set what he calls a financial finish line, and the overflow has fueled the Kingdom for decades.

The Lesson: I'm not saying that if you start tithing, someone will stop you on the street with a duffel bag of cash. I *am* saying that if you test God in this, He will do more than you can ask or think. Giving isn't where wealth goes to die. In the right hands, it's where wealth comes alive.

✦ ✦ ✦

Habit 6

The Habit of Going the Extra Mile

David and Jason Benham — twins, entrepreneurs, former pro baseball players — learned a defining habit young. One day their dad took them to a Denny's. Not to eat. To *watch*. They stood outside with a small crowd, looking in. Then a busboy in his fifties came to a dirty table, glanced at his watch, and went to work like a whirlwind — dishes and trash cleared, every inch wiped, everything in its place. He finished, checked his watch with a smile, and strolled off. The crowd at the window *applauded.*

Their dad turned to them: *"Every job is sacred. Every job is worthy of your best effort. You make it the best you can and turn it into something people cheer about — because your effort inspires them."*

The Benhams have used that principle ever since. In Little League they cleaned the dugout after every game. In the pros, Jason — a professional baseball player — helped the clubhouse manager do laundry, iron uniforms, and clean shoes. When a printing-company owner gave them a one-day job stacking pallets, they finished in four hours *and* cleaned his messy warehouse on top of it. When a banker faxed over a foreclosure job expecting it done in three days, they did it in two hours.

The Power of Going the Extra Mile

> *"And whosoever shall compel thee to go a mile, go with him twain."* (Matthew 5:41 NKJV)*

Jesus said this against the backdrop of an oppressive custom: under Persian and later Roman rule, an official could *compel* an ordinary person into service — Simon of Cyrene was compelled to carry Jesus' cross. Rather than tell us to resent it, Jesus said *exceed* it — go the second mile in a spirit of love.

But beyond Christian duty, the extra mile is a *powerful promotional tool.* The spotlight of comparison always shines on the person who uses it. They become indispensable. Why? Because in contrast, most people don't go even the first mile — and if they do, they go with a bad attitude.

Folorunsho Alakija knows this. She built a major fortune in the oil industry and became one of the wealthiest women in Africa — but she started as a secretary. Her father wouldn't send her to law school; he sent her to secretarial school instead. Frustrated but determined, she rose through the ranks of a bank — secretary, then corporate affairs, then the treasury — by relentlessly going the extra mile. Her take on "luck": "you *create* lucky by working extremely hard and going the extra mile. Especially, she added, as a woman who had to put in triple the effort just to be noticed."

More vs. Better: The Habit of Excellence

The extra mile is about doing *more*. But there's a close cousin worth naming: **excellence** — doing it *better*. Paul said it like this, *"And whatsoever ye do, do it heartily, as to the Lord, and not unto men." (Colossians 3:23 KJV)*

Daniel was promoted over an entire kingdom for one reason: *"because an excellent spirit was in him"* (Daniel 6:3). Excellence is what earns the premium and builds the reputation. The extra-miler shows up when others won't; the excellent one delivers what others can't. Do both, and you become not just indispensable but *irreplaceable.*

Not where you want to be yet? Not seeing the success you want? **Good.** Start using the habit nearly every Christian millionaire used. Go the extra mile — and do it with excellence.

✦ ✦ ✦

Habit 7

The Habit of Being Industrious

So you've prayed. You've found your niche. But you don't have enough help, money, or time. Do you just chalk it up?

Not quite. Here's where we grit it out and *make something happen.*

"Mike, that doesn't sound very godly. Aren't we supposed to wait on the Lord?" Yes — and no. There's a time to wait and be spiritual, and a time to be gritty and practical. Wisdom knows the difference. Even God said so:

> *"Then the Lord said to Moses, 'Quit praying and get the people moving! Forward, march!'" (Exodus 14:15 TLB)*

To be industrious is to be diligent, hardworking, and to make a way where there is no way. It's taking less and doing more with it.

Case in Point: Philip Anschutz

Anschutz is worth billions — but he started broke. In his mid-twenties he took over his father's struggling oil-drilling business, and by 27 he was nearly wiped out. Then in 1967 a rig hit a massive blowout near Gillette, Wyoming. Anschutz had the wells capped and got the idea to quietly buy up the surrounding oil leases on credit before anyone knew what was there.

Then came the bad news: a huge oil *fire*. He was convinced he was ruined. The famed firefighter Red Adair didn't even want the job — "Kid, I checked you out, and you don't check out." Anschutz pleaded. Adair relented. But now Anschutz had a field on fire, leases bought on credit, and no money to pay the firefighter.

What did he do? He got **industrious.** He learned Universal Studios was making a movie about Adair — so he negotiated a deal to let them film the crews fighting *his* fire for $100,000, enough to keep him afloat. The footage became part of the 1968 John Wayne film *Hellfighters*. That cash carried him to the next gusher — and years later he sold a stake in one field to Mobil for half a billion dollars.

A lot of great things happen to industrious people. Jesus spoke about someone who needed to be industrious at the right time:

> *"Now here's a surprise: The master praised the crooked manager! And why? Because he knew how to look after himself. Streetwise people are smarter in this regard than law-abiding citizens. They are on constant alert, looking for angles, surviving by their wits. I want you to be smart in the same way—but for what is right—using every adversity to stimulate you to creative survival, to concentrate your attention on the bare essentials, so you'll live, really live, and not complacently just get by on good behavior." (Luke 16:8–9 MSG)*

Truett Cathy's Scrappy Start

S. Truett Cathy, the founder of Chick-fil-A, knew the value of industriousness. When he and his brother opened their first restaurant, they underestimated the cost — and solved each shortage creatively:

- Short on nails? They drove to small towns to find them and straightened bent ones.
- Short on lumber? They scavenged scrap wood from torn-down buildings.
- Couldn't afford restaurant equipment? They bought used gear from failed restaurants.
- Couldn't afford skilled labor? They hung the sheetrock and dug the footings themselves.

- Couldn't get meat? They asked a larger local restaurant with supplier access to buy it for them.

That scrappiness seeded a company now doing many billions in annual sales — built on a foundation of doing much with little.

The bottom line: Don't have enough to work with? Great. Learn to be industrious — *now.*

✦ ✦ ✦

Habit 8

The Habit of Holy Risk

The Parable of the Talents

Here's a question that exposes your mindset faster than any other: **what do you do with what you've been given when there's a chance you could lose it?**

Jesus answered it with a story.

> *"For the kingdom of heaven is as a man travelling into a far country, who called his own servants, and delivered unto them his goods. And unto one he gave five talents, to another two, and to another one... Then he that had received the five talents went and traded with the same, and made them other five talents."* (Matthew 25:14–16 KJV)*

Two servants *put their master's money to work* and doubled it. The third did something that sounds safe and responsible: he buried it. He protected it. He took no risk.

And the master called him **wicked and slothful.** He took the one talent away and gave it to the man who had ten.

Read that again, because it's the opposite of what religion often teaches. The servant who played it safe out of *fear* was condemned. The servants who *risked* and multiplied were rewarded. Why? Listen to the buried-talent servant's own words: *"I was afraid, and went and hid thy talent."* (Matthew 25:25)

Fear. Scarcity. "I'd better protect what little I have."

That's a poverty mindset — and God will not bless a buried talent.

Abundance Takes Holy Risks

This is where the mindset of Part One meets the hands of Part Two. The abundant mind doesn't bury — it *deploys*. It sees that everything already belongs to God anyway, that He is a good Master, and so it can take bold, prayerful, calculated risks without being ruled by fear.

You've already met two men who lived this:

Philip Anschutz bought oil leases *on credit* — money he didn't have — betting on what he believed was under the ground. That's not recklessness; that's a calculated, faith-backed risk. The buried-talent man would have done nothing and stayed broke.

Strive Masiyiwa — whose full story is coming — bet his entire, already-successful electrical company against a corrupt government to chase a vision of wireless telephones, when everyone said it couldn't be done. He risked it all. And as you'll see, he won.

Even David Green, when his company teetered near bankruptcy, didn't bury his head — he made the bold, prayerful bet to get back to his core and rebuild, rather than fold.

Holy Risk Is Not Recklessness

Hear me clearly: this is not a license to gamble, to go into foolish debt, or to "name it and claim it" your way into a bad decision. Holy risk is *prayerful, counseled* (remember Habit 3), and *stewarded*. It's the difference between throwing your money on a table in Vegas and planting a seed in a field you've studied and prayed over.

But make no mistake — there is *no harvest without a planted seed*, and there is no seed planted without the willingness to let it leave your hand and go into the ground.

> *"He which soweth sparingly shall reap also sparingly; and he which soweth bountifully shall reap also bountifully."(2 Corinthians 9:6 KJV)*

The Lesson: Stop burying your talent. Whatever God has put in your hand — money, a skill, an idea, an opportunity — He gave it to you to *multiply*, not to protect out of fear. Pray over it. Get counsel on it. Then take the holy risk. The Master is not impressed by the safe servant. He's looking for the ones who put His goods to work.

✦ ✦ ✦

Habit 9

The Habit of Managing Money Well

Most people pray for increase. Few realize that real increase comes by way of proper *management*. God is not wasteful, and He doesn't hand *more* to people who haven't proven they can handle *less*.

Look closely at the creation account:

> *"...the LORD God had not caused it to rain upon the earth, and there was not a man to till the ground." (Genesis 2:5 KJV)*

Did you catch that? God didn't send the rain because there was no man to *work* or no man-*ager*. In God's economy: **no management, no increase.** But proper management leads to proper increase.

Rockefeller and the Drop of Solder

Rockefeller, the richest Christian to date, *hated* waste. As a young man he paid a dime for a small red book, called it Ledger A, and recorded every receipt and expense to the penny. That habit followed him everywhere.

Once, inspecting a plant that sealed five-gallon cans of kerosene, he watched a machine solder caps onto cans and asked how many drops of solder it used. "Forty," the expert said. Rockefeller asked him to try thirty-eight. At thirty-eight, the cans leaked. At thirty-nine, they didn't. So thirty-nine became the standard. That one drop saved $2,500 the first year — and as the business multiplied, it added up to hundreds of thousands.

Pennies managed properly give birth to beautiful dollars.

Seed vs. Harvest

During their lean years, the Benham brothers figured each family needed about $1,500 a month to survive. They found a $210,000 home selling for $150,000 and moved *both* families in — four adults and three kids under five. Tight? Painfully. But even as the business grew, they kept living small on purpose. As they put it, the money earned in a business's early years is *seed* money — it belongs back in the ground. Too many owners treat early earnings as *harvest* and reap it prematurely. That, they said, is why so many businesses fail in the first five years.

Build Debt-Free — and Reinvest: The David Green Model

Here's where I want to update the playbook. We usually talk about debt *defensively* — get out of it (and we will). But David Green shows the *offensive* power of refusing it in the first place.

Hobby Lobby is run, famously, almost entirely **debt-free.** Green opens dozens of new stores every single year — and funds that growth out of *cash flow,* not loans. No bank can call his note. No creditor owns a piece of his upside. When the rest of retail is leveraged to the eyeballs and panics in a downturn, a debt-free company keeps building. Slower at the start, maybe. But it *compounds,* and it *owns 100% of what it builds.* That's not just safe. It's a strategy.

Become Financially Literate

Passion and startup cash aren't enough. If you don't have the financial skills yourself, partner with someone who does — but never hand your business to an accountant and look away. Know exactly where your company stands at all times. The Bible says,

"Be thou diligent to know the state of thy flocks, and look well to thy herds." (Proverbs 27:23 KJV)

In an agricultural world, flocks were wealth. To know their state was to know your income and expenses. Translation: be financially literate. Know your numbers.

Money: A Better Slave Than Master

When he was twelve years old the young Rockefeller had saved $50 and loaned it to a farmer at 7% interest. He learned early that it was better to make money his *slave* than to be its servant. He was always putting money to work. Jesus said it like this, *"Occupy till I come." (Luke 19:13 KJV)*

That word **"occupy"** is the Greek **"diapragmateuomai"** – "to gain by trading," "to be busily engaged in making trades," "to increase by trading." In other words: *put it to work and multiply it until I come.* (And if you want the fuller teaching on the holy risk that multiplication requires, you just read it in Habit 8.)

Get Out of Debt – Now

One of the greatest hindrances to a future Christian millionaire is debt. Debt isn't a sin, but it *is* a master:

> *"The rich ruleth over the poor, and the borrower is servant to the lender."* (Proverbs 22:7 KJV)*
>
> *"Owe no man any thing, but to love one another."* (Romans 13:8 KJV)*

Just ask Gary Keesee. We met his debt mountain already. There was a night it all came to a head – he had one credit card that wasn't maxed, used it for gas and gas-station food, was so rattled with relief the card went through that he drove off with the pump still in the tank and ripped the hose clean off. The humiliation, he said, was unlike anything he'd felt.

When an attorney called demanding money they didn't have, Gary collapsed on his bed to pray – and realized the truth: he trusted *debt* more than he trusted God. He repented to his wife Drenda, and they made a cold-turkey commitment: no more debt, period. "If we go down, we go down – and they can write on our tombstone, *they went down trusting God.*"

That commitment got tested fast. Their van burned up. Insurance paid it off and left a little cash — but now they had no vehicle. Gary's father offered to co-sign a new van; after prayer, they declined, refusing new debt. Then Drenda, selling antiques on the side, closed a $500 furniture deal she'd left a message about *before* the van burned, and traded the commission for a good used car. Suddenly: a paid-for car, a credit card cleared, the van loan settled. "So trusting God *does* work," they said. That's the lesson that birthed their debt-help business — and within two and a half years they were debt-free themselves.

Your assignment:

- **Audit your management.** Are you tracking income and expenses? Do you have a budget? If not, stop asking God for more — He gives His best resources to His wisest stewards.
- **Make a plan to get out of debt.** (A system like Dave Ramsey's works well.)
- **Make a plan to *multiply* your money.** Clipping coupons isn't stewardship's finish line. God's stewards *multiply* and give back — and those are the stewards who get the bulk of His resources.

✦ ✦ ✦

Habit 10

The Habit of Persistence

Strive Masiyiwa is Zimbabwe's first billionaire — a respected businessman known for his social conscience, philanthropy, and mentorship of younger entrepreneurs. But before the accolades, he was an idealist fighting a brutally uphill battle against a corrupt government.

In the 1980s he ran his own electrical contracting firm — a multimillion-dollar national company with close to 500 employees. Then he spotted both a problem and an opportunity: the region had almost no telephones, and wireless networks would be faster, cheaper, and harder to sabotage than landlines. He went to the state phone company about building a mobile network. They weren't interested — the mobile phone "had no future," they said. The real reason ran deeper: under Robert Mugabe, the government didn't want private citizens to have private communications.

Here was his dilemma. He had a constitutional right to start a mobile company — freedom of expression included the right to receive and impart information. But if he proceeded, the government threatened to prosecute him *and* to sever all contracts with his existing firm, its biggest client.

He moved forward anyway. When his wife asked how long it would take, he said, "Three to four months." It took nearly **five years.**

Persistence — and the Integrity Underneath It

The cost was devastating. The government did cancel his contracts — within months he could barely make payroll. He sold off company assets to fund the legal fight. At one point, his wife said, they were so broke they couldn't afford to offer visitors tea.

But here's the piece I want you to see, because it's a wealth principle hiding inside a persistence story: **Masiyiwa would not compromise to win.** He refused to play the corrupt game — refused the bribes and the back-room deals that "everyone" used to grease licenses in that era. That integrity is *exactly* what made the fight so long and so expensive. The short, cheap road was available. He wouldn't take it.

And in December 1997, the Zimbabwean Supreme Court awarded his company — Econet — its license, ruling the government's monopoly violated freedom of communication. Econet launched in 1998 and within months became the country's leading mobile telecom. Today it spans much of a continent.

The lesson is double: persistence won the war — *and* the integrity he refused to surrender is what made the victory clean, durable, and trusted. The expensive "no" early became the unshakable reputation later. Paul was very clear about this: *"And let us not be weary in well doing: for in due season we shall reap, if we faint not."* (Galatians 6:9 KJV)*

The Bulldog: Folorunsho Alakija (Again)

We met Alakija going the extra mile. Her *defining* quality, though, is pit-bull determination. She does not give up.

When she moved into oil, doors slammed in her face. She kept knocking. Told her input wasn't wanted — she kept investigating. Her license application got shelved — she kept applying. After three years, she was finally granted an oil bloc that *no other company wanted.* She took it anyway. When her technical partners pulled out, she and her husband poured their life savings in and hunted for new ones. Three more years — then they struck oil in commercial quantity.

A storybook ending? Not yet. Once the bloc proved valuable, the government seized a large stake. Friends and officials told her to be grateful for what she had left and walk away. Instead, she fought — in court, for **twelve years.** Sleepless nights, isolation, enormous stakes. And in the end she won — because she was right, because justice was on her side, because of the favor of God, and because, like any bulldog, she refused to give up her bone.

No outstanding achievement is won without continuous effort. The wheel of fortune turns slowly, and it turns toward those who've proven, through persistence, that they deserve its rewards. Before *anyone* meets *any* success, they first meet misfortune, mistakes, delays, and temporary defeat.

But there's something about a persistent person that makes God smile.

PART THREE — THE LEGACY

Wealth That Outlives You

✦ ✦ ✦

Habit 11

The Habit of Creating Value at Scale

Let me tell you the real secret behind every fortune in this book — the one that ties them all together.

Wealth flows to the one who solves the biggest problem for the most people.

That's it. Strip away the industries and the eras, and that's the engine. Rockefeller didn't get rich hoarding oil; he got rich making energy cheap and available to millions. The Changs (in their rising years) clothed a generation. Masiyiwa connected a continent that had two phones per hundred people. Anschutz, Cathy, Green — every one of them got paid in proportion to the size of the problem they solved and the number of people they served.

This is not a worldly idea. It's a Kingdom one.

Joseph: Wealth That Saved Nations

When Pharaoh dreamed of seven years of plenty and seven of famine, God gave Joseph not just the interpretation but a *plan* — store grain at scale through the good years to feed the world through the bad ones.

> *"And Joseph gathered corn as the sand of the sea, very much, until he left numbering; for it was without number."* (Genesis 41:49 KJV)*

Joseph's management created value at a scale that saved Egypt, his own family, and *"all countries"* that came to buy grain. His wealth and authority weren't the point — they were the *byproduct* of solving a problem big enough to rescue nations. The bigger the problem he was trusted to solve, the more he was given to steward.

Solomon's kingdom grew fabulously wealthy the same way — through trade, wisdom, and enterprise that served and enriched a whole nation.

Modern Scale, Same Principle

David Steward didn't just build a fortune; he built World Wide Technology into a company employing thousands and serving some of the largest organizations on earth — value at scale. David Green's Hobby Lobby provides tens of thousands of jobs. Truett Cathy's restaurants feed millions and put thousands of young people through their first responsible work.

See the pattern? **The wealth tracked the service.** These weren't people chasing dollars. They were people who asked, "How big a problem can I solve? How many people can I serve?" — and the dollars came chasing *them*. Jesus said it like this, *"Whosoever will be great among you, let him be your minister." (Matthew 20:26 KJV)*

That word "minister" means *servant*. In the Kingdom, the path to greatness — and to great resources — runs straight through great service.

The Lesson: Stop asking, "How do I make more money?" Start asking, "Whose problem can I solve, and for how many?" Build something that serves at scale, and you build something that *pays* at scale. Wealth in good hands is simply service that grew large. This is why wealth is a good thing in the hands of the godly — because a lot of it, deployed well, does a *lot* of good.

✦ ✦ ✦

Habit 12

The Habit of Leaving an Inheritance

We end here on purpose. Because the goal was never the size of your bank account on the day you die. The goal is what *outlives* you.

> *"A good man leaveth an inheritance to his children's children: and the wealth of the sinner is laid up for the just."* (Proverbs 13:22 KJV)*

Look closely. Not just an inheritance to your children — to your children's *children.* A good man thinks in *generations.* He builds something so durable, so well-stewarded, that it blesses people he will never meet. That is the final habit, and it's the one that turns a rich man into a patriarch.

The Green Family: A Legacy by Design

David Green didn't just build Hobby Lobby — he built it to *last past him,* debt-free, on biblical principles, with the values written into the company's DNA. And he handed his children not only a business but a *mission.* His son **Mart Green** runs Mardel, a Christian retail chain — and helped found Every Tribe Every Nation, a global effort to get Scripture translated into every remaining language on earth. The Greens have poured enormous resources into the Museum of the Bible and ministries worldwide.

That's the difference between a fortune and a *legacy.* A fortune is what you spend. A legacy is what keeps giving after you're gone — across generations, across the world.

Barnhart's Trust: Giving That Won't Stop

Remember Alan Barnhart, who gave his company into a charitable trust? Think about what he actually did: he built a structure so that the wealth keeps flowing to the Kingdom *whether he's alive or not*. He didn't just give — he built a *machine* for giving that outlives him. That is inheritance thinking at its highest: not "what will I leave my kids," but "what will I leave *running* for generations."

You Are a Link in a Chain

Here's the mindset shift that crowns this whole book. You are not the destination of God's blessing. You are a *conduit* of it — a link in a chain that stretches back to Abraham and forward to people not yet born.

> *"I will make of thee a great nation, and I will bless thee... and thou shalt be a blessing... and in thee shall all families of the earth be blessed."* (Genesis 12:2–3 KJV)*

Blessed to be a blessing. You become great so that others — your children, their children, your community, the nations — become great too. The wealth you build in good hands isn't a trophy to clutch. It's a torch to pass.

The Lesson: Build like someone is coming after you. Get out of debt so you don't pass on bondage. Multiply so there's something to pass on. Teach your children the secrets in this book so the habits outlive the money. And, like the wisest of these millionaires, build *structures* — trusts, businesses, ministries — that keep blessing the world long after you've gone home.

Leave an inheritance to your children's children. That's not greed. That's godliness with a long view.

Conclusion

Go Be Great

One day, walking, Jesus was followed by two blind men crying out for mercy — they wanted to see. After a brief exchange, *"He touched their eyes... saying... According to your faith be it unto you"* or as one translation puts it, *"Become what you believe."* (Matthew 9:29 MSG)

It's my hope that after reading this, you become what you were meant to be — and *become what you believe.*

Know this: you were meant to be great.

But the definition of greatness is as varied as the people who chase it. In spite of all the definitions, one thing characterizes *true* greatness: **service.** To serve is to be great.

> *"Don't push your way to the front; don't sweet-talk your way to the top. Put yourself aside, and help others get ahead... Forget yourselves long enough to lend a helping hand." (Philippians 2:3–4 MSG)*

True greatness was never about being great at the *expense* of others — but at the expense of *self.* We were all meant to be great because we were all meant to serve. And now you know the secret behind the secret: these habits don't just make millionaires. They make *blessings* — people whose wealth, in good hands, lifts everyone around them and everyone who comes after them.

You found the secrets. Now make them habits.

Then go be great.

Resources

The following books, interviews, and sources informed the stories and principles in this book.

Introduction

- New World Wealth / CNBC: "The Religion of Millionaires" — wealth and faith demographics research.
- Do Won & Jin Sook Chang / Forever 21: founding biography and company history.
- Gary & Drenda Keesee: *Fixing the Money Thing* (Harrison House); *She Gets It* (Harrison House). Charisma News profile of Drenda Keesee.
- Steven K. Scott: *The Richest Man Who Ever Lived* (WaterBrook Press).

Habit 1 — Seeking God First

- Do Won & Jin Sook Chang: Forever 21 founding story; Linda Chang quoted in company profile.
- Jason & David Benham: *Whatever the Cost* (Thomas Nelson).
- Gary & Drenda Keesee: *Fixing the Money Thing* (Harrison House).
- David Steward: *Doing Business by the Good Book* (Hyperion).

Habit 2 — Gratitude / The Law of Thanksgiving

- John D. Rockefeller: Ron Chernow, *Titan: The Life of John D. Rockefeller, Sr.* (Random House).

- Sir John Templeton: *Worldwide Laws of Life* (Templeton Foundation Press).

Habit 3 — The Big Vision

- Steven K. Scott: *The Richest Man Who Ever Lived* (WaterBrook Press); church conference talk on "shooting for the moon."
- Simon Sinek: "Start With Why," TED Talk, 2009.

Habit 4 — Purpose / Staying in Your Sphere

- David Green: *Giving It All Away...and Getting It All Back Again* (Zondervan).
- Do Won & Jin Sook Chang: Forever 21 bankruptcy filings, 2019 and 2025 (Reuters; AP; CNBC).

Habit 5 — Giving

- John D. Rockefeller: *Titan* (Random House).
- Chantel Ray: CBN, "From Buying Groceries on Credit to a Multi-Million-Dollar Business."
- State of the Plate tithing research: stateoftheplate.info (research across 5,444 Christians).
- Alan Barnhart: Generous Giving testimonials and interviews; Barnhart Crane & Rigging company history.

Habit 6 — Going the Extra Mile

- Jason & David Benham: *Whatever the Cost* (Thomas Nelson).
- Folorunsho Alakija: CNBC Africa, "How Africa's Second-Richest Woman Gained Her Fortune"; ALD interview.

Habit 7 — Being Industrious

- Philip Anschutz: Fortune, "The Billionaire Next Door."
- S. Truett Cathy: Chick-fil-A company history and press materials.

Habit 8 — Holy Risk

- Matthew 25:14–30 (KJV): The Parable of the Talents.

Habit 9 — Managing Money Well

- John D. Rockefeller: *Titan* (Random House).
- Jason & David Benham: *Whatever the Cost* (Thomas Nelson).
- David Green: *More Than a Hobby* (Thomas Nelson); *Giving It All Away* (Zondervan).
- Pete Leonard / I Have a Bean: Huffington Post, "5 Innovative Christian Businesses You've Probably Never Heard Of."
- Gary & Drenda Keesee: *Fixing the Money Thing* (Harrison House).

Habit 10 — Persistence

- Strive Masiyiwa: Econet Wireless blog, "Lessons from the Early Days"; Tsitsi Masiyiwa interview, "Wealth, Marriage & Philanthropy."
- Folorunsho Alakija: CNBC Africa profile; ALD interview.

Habit 12 — Leaving an Inheritance

- Mart Green: Every Tribe Every Nation (everytribeeverynation.org); Museum of the Bible.
- Alan Barnhart: Generous Giving testimonials.

BOOK TWO

THE RICHEST MAN IN CHURCH

A Novel

Michael Holmes

Chapter 1 - Wretched Man

"But there is something else deep within me, in my lower nature, that is at war with my mind and wins the fight and makes me a slave to the sin that is still within me. In my mind, I want to be God's willing servant, but instead, I find myself still enslaved to sin." [1]

"Why do I keep doing this?"

DeMarcus looks up at the ceiling in the bedroom he's grown accustomed to, and in that bed lies the girl he shouldn't be accustomed to.

Familiar story: lust in the evening, guilt in the morning.

DeMarcus at 21 years of age was a Christian man. He went to church religiously; he believed sexual immorality was wrong, but he couldn't stop himself from it and truth is, he didn't want to.

"Mmmmm," said the girl lying next to him as she stretched. "You awake baby?"

Her name: Ebony. Everything about her seduced him; no matter how many times he had her, it was never enough. She was his weakness, his Achilles heel, his Delilah. Her brown skin, naturally curly hair, soft lips, the way she walked into a room, and the presence she brought with her...everything...absolutely everything about her mesmerized him.

"Yeah, I'm awake," DeMarcus said, still lost in his thoughts. Still wondering how many times he would fail, apologize, "repent," and end up doing the same thing over.

She turned over and slid next to him. Then pulled off the blanket and said, "I'll be back." She walked off naked to the bathroom.

Her naked, shapely, and smooth body took his mind off his eternal dilemma. "God, she's gorgeous," he thought to himself. He looked up again at the ceiling; a sea of thoughts crashed against the shores of his mind:

"If God didn't want me to do this, why didn't He take my desire away?"

"Why is this so bad?"

"God, she's good. And THAT thing she did last night...omg!"

"What time do I have to get to work?"

"Awww shoot...mom!"

He grabbed his phone to see the time and check his messages. He didn't mean to fall asleep there. The intent was to come over, talk, and head out. That didn't end up well.

He scrolled through his text messages to see that his mother called, left a voice message, and texted him. His mom was in his estimation, the best mom ever. But even he knew she had her limits. He texted her:

"Sorry mom, I fell asleep at a friend's house. I. am. sorry."

He put the phone down. He knew he was in trouble, but nothing he could do about it now. He'd have to cross that bridge when he got there. Just then he could hear the toilet flush, the water in the sink running, and then the door opened. She walked into the room, pulled up the covers, and slid next to him again. "God, she feels good!" he thought.

"So how did you sleep?" she asked.

"I slept well. I can't complain."

"I'm sure you did with all that work you put in last night," she said as she kissed his neck. He could smell the cool mint Listerine on her breath; just then, he realized he needed to use the bathroom himself. So he pulled off the covers, found his boxers, stood up, and was about to put them on.

"No," Ebony interrupted him. "I want to see what's mine. Don't hide it."

She laughed and he smiled as he threw the boxers to the ground. He loved her personality, he loved the fact he could talk to her about most things, but she didn't believe in God, the Bible, and the church as he did.

She considered it a crutch. "It's something the white man gave to Black people to keep them submissive," she said. He hated the fact that he was not acting the way of a "model" Christian. His faith had little substance and he knew it.

He walked to the bathroom, used it, brushed his teeth with the toothbrush she bought for him, washed his hands, and walked back to the bed. He pulled the covers and lay next to her.

"What time do you have to go to work?" DeMarcus asked.

"Oh...you trying to get rid of me, DeMarcus?" she asked with a chuckle. "Remember I told you today is a later day. I'm starting later and am going to end later. That's why I wanted you to come over last night."

"Oh...so you PLANNED to take advantage of me?" he asked with a slight grin.

“I meeeaaan... were you really disadvantaged?” She said as she slid her body closer to his. She put her hand on his stomach and kissed him on his neck. “Seems like you need another lesson on ‘advantages’ and ‘disadvantages.’”

“You know what...maybe it’s time I got going,” DeMarcus said.

“DeMarcus,” Ebony started as she slid her hand down further. “Are you REALLY trying to leave now?”

He knew it was wrong, but the will of God was going to have to take a backseat on this. He kissed her and started a journey with his own hands.

Chapter 2 - Backdrop

It was 9am when DeMarcus left Ebony's apartment. It was a 20 minute walk back to his place. It gave him the time to think, ponder, and wonder how he was going to explain to his mom his absence.

He is the son of Marcus and Delores Watson. His name means "of Marcus" or "son of Marcus." "Marcus" means "polite" or "shining."

Things seem to spiral downward the most with his father's untimely death. His father was his hero. He was the bedrock of his family; He was loved by his wife, his community, and his church. He shone everywhere he went.

He particularly shone in his church: NY Christian Pentecostal Church. Marcus served as a deacon, but his influence was felt even further. He had an uncanny ability to make people feel welcome, beloved, and accepted. Even though he shunned the public spotlight, his influence was felt by all.

It was a sad day when he was diagnosed with lung cancer (ironic because he was NOT a smoker). It was even a darker day when he passed one month later.

There were no seats left on the day of his funeral and the Bishop had to stop people from saying a "few words" for the sake of time. Marcus was beloved and he was missed. But no two people felt that loss more than DeMarcus and Delores. Often DeMarcus would hear his mother crying in her room saying, "Lord why? Why him?"

With the loss of his hero DeMarcus just seemed to be drifting. On the surface, he seemed like any ordinary young man in the church. He attended church regularly. The theater of Pentecostalism was amusing to him: the sporadic tongue talking, the rhythmic music that gave way to dancing in the aisles, the overweight lady that would dance for a good while "under the spirit" but would slow down when her cardio gave way.

He loved his church, loved the community and fellowship it gave him, but there was one thing he needed that he didn't know he needed: mentorship.

I mean it was great to go over the Bible stories, but he needed tangible answers. The church gave him a warm community. But he needed direction - tangible direction.

He loved his pastor. He was a good man, a good leader, and a good preacher. He would start slow and end up preaching with gasps backed up by the organist's riffs: "And the Lord told me (huh) to tell youuuu (huh) that this is your YEAR (huh) your season (huh) your tiiiiiimmmmmmeeee!!!!"

But he needed more than words, promises, and the talk of his potential. He needed results. Results that he didn't seem to be having, and that frustration coupled with the effects of his double life was causing him to be more and more disillusioned with the church. His frustration was turning into apathy.

No one noticed the subtle changes except one woman: his mother.

Delores Naomi Watson was the daughter of a broken home. Her mother, who discarded any forms of tradition, had four different children with four different men. Delores never knew her father; she only heard of him. According to her mother, he was "no good just like the rest of 'em."

She always grew up with an unspoken conversation she wanted to have with her mother: “Mama if THEY no good, why do you keep laying up with them?” But experience told her that conversation needed to stay in her head.

As she ventured out into her version of adulthood, she found herself following the footsteps of her mama; minus the kids. Liquor, men, and endless parties were leading her down a path she didn’t like and didn’t have the strength to come back from. She was trapped and she knew it.

One Sunday morning after another wild night of partying (she didn't know how she got home) she woke up and knew she needed to change. “God, help me,” she prayed.

She sat there for a while, wondering what to do next, and all of a sudden she thought about a storefront church she occasionally passed: Christian Pentecostal Church. She hadn’t been to church in years, but at that moment, she felt the urge to go.

She came late and sat on the backbench. The ushers motioned for her to go to the front. She refused. “I don’t know y’all; why would I go to the front?” she said to herself.

A man got up (the man who would later become her Bishop) and said that God told him he needed to preach from the Song of Solomon. “Song of What?” Delores said to herself. “Who is Solomon? And how are you gonna ‘preach’ from his lyrics??”

It wasn't until he opened his Bible that Delores understood. He read a passage:

“By night on my bed I sought him whom my soul loveth: I sought him, but I found him not.

I will rise now, and go about the city In the streets, and in the broad ways, I will seek him whom my soul loveth: I sought him, but I found him not.

The watchmen that go about the city found me: To whom I said, 'Saw ye him whom my soul loveth? It was but a little that I passed from them, But I found him whom my soul loveth: I held him, and would not let him go, Until I had brought him into my mother's house, And into the chamber of her that conceived me.'" [1]

After he closed the Bible and spoke, it seemed as if he were speaking directly to her. He said, "Some of you are looking for love in places where you won't find it. This woman couldn't find it in her home so she looked in the streets. And she looked all up and down the streets even in broad ways, but she couldn't find it. And then she came to the watchman. Let me tell you something. I'm that watchman and I'm going about this city to tell YOU about a Man! No, He's not a man from the club. Here to wine you, dine you, and forget about you!

"No, no, no saints of God...He's bigger than a church and greater than a preacher. The Bible said that when this woman got beyond the watchmen, church, and organized religion she found that man. I'm here to tell you... saints of God... that Man's Name is Jesus!!!"

"He said, 'Come unto me, all ye that labor and are heavy laden, and I will give you rest. Take My yoke upon you, and learn of Me; for I am meek and lowly in heart: and ye shall find rest unto your souls.' [2]

"You not gonna find this rest in a bottle (huh), you not gonna find this rest in the club (huh), you not gonna find this rest in some stranger's bed (huh). You only gonna find this rest with Jesus...the Alpha and the Omega (huh)...JESUS...the bright and morning star...JESUS...the lily of the valley!!! Somebody say "yes"!!![3], [4], [5]

By this, tears were streaming down Delores' face. She WAS that woman and she knew she needed to change. She needed God. She just didn't know what to do next.

An usher and "mother" in the church, Sis. Veronica Davis saw Delores' face out of the corner of her eye. She had enough insight to know that God was doing something in Delores' heart. She walked over to Delores and softly put her hands on her shoulders.

"Hey, baby," Sis. Davis started. "Did you need prayer?"

"Yes ma'am," Delores said, barely holding back her tears.

"Ok baby follow me."

With the motherly care Delores had been craving all her life, Sis. Davis tenderly guided her to the altar. They sat down together.

"Baby, do you want Jesus to come into your heart?" Sis Davis asked.

"I don't know...will He accept me?" Delores asked.

"He brought you here baby. He loves you. And He's already accepted you. Will you accept Him?"

With that, more tears poured forward. "Yes ma'am."

Sis. Davis led Delores in the sinners' prayer; It seemed like a 1,000 pound weight was lifted off Delores' shoulders. She couldn't explain it, but she felt free.

Delores could still remember that day vividly, and she reflected on the events that transpired after: her giving up the nightlife, the men and friends she said goodbye to, the ridicule from her mother, her baptism, her inclusion into that particular church body, her Bible readings, her service in the church and community, her introduction to a particularly handsome young man named Marcus, their friendship, courtship, marriage, and them creating the miracle of DeMarcus.

It seemed like yesterday and, at the same time, felt like an eternity. She marveled at how far God had brought her. She thought about all the hardships He brought her through, the miracles He had accomplished in her life, and the family He put her in.

She thought about all this as she sat patiently waiting for her son.

She thought about this as she grappled with her emotions: anger, fear, disappointment. Since no one can really understand the depth of a mother's love and understanding, she knew something was off. She knew something was off with his walk with Dad (her name for God).

She'd been up praying since 7am this morning. She needed an answer and Dad was her only option. She combed through Scriptures, mediated on them, and listened intently for Dad's Voice. She needed a strategy because she knew nagging wasn't an option. Originally, when she got his text, the only thing she felt was rage. How could he? What "friend" allowed him to stay over the entire night? Was he drunk? Was he sick? Was he in a fight? All these questions swirled through her mind. These same questions and frustrations she vented to Dad.

Two Scriptures seemed to come back to her:

"Or despisest thou the riches of his goodness and forbearance and longsuffering; not knowing that the goodness of God leadeth thee to repentance?" [6]

"Grandchildren are the crown of the aged, and the glory of a son is his father." [7]

Regarding the first, she realized anger would be counterproductive. Her nagging him or shouting at him was not the answer...this time. When he came in the door, she was going to show him kindness. Daddy was kind to her when she messed up; it was her time to do the same for her son.

Regarding the second, she realized some significant changes had taken place since Marcus passed. DeMarcus needed his father. She couldn't reach him as his father did. Who could? Just then she heard his key in the door.

DeMarcus tried to sneak in quietly but was startled to see his mom staring at him in the living room.

"Mom! I uh..." he started flabbergasted.

She held up her hand. "Are you ok?" she asked.

"Yes ma'am."

"Are you hurt?"

"No ma'am."

"Is anyone else hurt?"

"No ma'am."

She took a deep breath, stood up, walked towards him, and hugged him. He stood there motionless, unsure of what to do next.

“You apologized,” she started. “You’re alive. No one is hurt. But... DO NOT let this happen again.” She looked him straight in the eye for emphasis. Then she walked off. “Don’t you have to get ready for work?”

“Uhhh,” he stood there stunned. “Yes ma’am.”

DeMarcus couldn’t believe what had just taken place. He felt even worse for putting his mom through that. His admiration for her grew even more. “Never again,” he silently vowed to himself.

Delores however, was in deep thought as she went to her room and closed the door. She was proud of herself because everything in her wanted to rip him to shreds, but she knew her obedience had to be greater than her feelings.

But she knew more was needed. She knew there had to be a MAN who could reach him.

“Dad, what do I do?” she prayed. “If I can’t reach him, who can?”

Suddenly a face flashed in her mind.

Could it be? Could he be the one? I mean, he was a good man, respectable, and highly respected. Could he be the one to help DeMarcus in his walk with God? Could he assist him in his walk towards manhood?

Would he do it? Would his wife allow the mentorship? Would it help?

“Well,” she said to herself. “We don't have because we don’t ask.”

Delores found her cell and because she had a good relationship with his wife, she called her first.

"Candice, good morning. How are you, my sister? Good. Good. We're all good thank God. How is George? And the kids? Thank God. Listen...is it possible to have some coffee with you and George? It's something I want to talk to you two about. It's regarding DeMarcus..."

Chapter 3 - The Meeting

DeMarcus worked in the bookstore of NY Christian Pentecostal Church. The church by this time had grown from a storefront to a burgeoning mega-church. It had staff, budgets, and for-profit businesses. Even though there were critics who said a church shouldn't have for-profit businesses, the Bishop was adamant this was a necessity. He didn't want to rely solely on tithes and offerings. "If there is no margin, there is no mission" he would often say.

The bookstore job that DeMarcus had paid the little bills he had. But it wasn't challenging or fulfilling nor was he winning awards for being an employee of the year. He did duties but only that: his duties. He did no less and DEFINITELY did no more.

It had been three and a half weeks since the incident of staying out all night. Even though his meetings with Ebony didn't cease entirely - he never stayed the night again. He refused to put his mother through that experience again.

For the most part, DeMarcus' mind was on cruise control at the bookstore. He was restocking a shelf when a middle-aged man walked up to him.

"Excuse me," the man asked. "I'm looking for the Bible section."

"Well...you actually just passed it," DeMarcus said. He smiled but didn't really give the man his attention. "About three shelves behind me, you'll see all the Bibles."

"So I guess you don't believe in customer service, huh son?"

"Excuse me?" DeMarcus said, turning around to address the man.

The man looked to be in his mid to late forties. The only thing that gave away his age was the salt and pepper in his goatee. He was slender, about as tall as DeMarcus, and had brown penetrating eyes.

He seemed like a man who knew where he was going and didn't have time to waste.

"You heard me," the stranger responded. "You could've pointed me in the right direction, but you didn't even give me the respect of turning around. All I did was speak to your back. Do YOU think that's customer service?"

DeMarcus didn't know how to respond. He WAS right. But who was he to tell him about himself? He wasn't his dad. Who was he? A supervisor he didn't know about?

Then DeMarcus thought about his response: should he be upset? Nah, that wouldn't work. Technically he WAS right. Should he apologize? Nah, he might throw the apology in his face.

"Nothing to say? Hmmm...there might be hope for you yet," the stranger said. "I probably CAN teach you something."

"Look sir," DeMarcus started. "The Bibles are three shelves behind you. I'll walk you over there." He started to put the books he was shelving down.

"I'm just teasing you. I have enough Bibles. And I have enough books."

"Soooo...?" DeMarcus asked.

"My name is George, DeMarcus. It's a pleasure to meet you."

With that, George held out his hand. DeMarcus looked at the hand then looked at the man extending it. He cautiously shook his hand...still weirded out by the initial meeting. Who WAS this guy?

"Nice to meet you, George. Uh...what can I help you with?"

"Well DeMarcus you don't know me but I know you, I know your mom...and I knew your Dad. I was in the neighborhood and I was hoping you'd join me for a cup of coffee. Do you drink coffee?"

"Uh...I do. But for one: I don't know you. How do you know my parents?"

"Well, I'm a member of this church," George said. "You know that IS one of the problems of large churches: it can take away the community and family feel. And you're not really known unless you're preaching, singing, or speaking from the stage. But I've been here for quite a while."

"So let me get this straight," DeMarcus started. "You've known about me, known my family for years, never met me, but decided to introduce yourself by testing me on my customer service skills. Did I miss anything here George?"

George looked at him with those penetrating eyes. He had to admit: he respected his directness. He spoke his truth. In a world of carbon copies, it was refreshing to see a possible great original.

"You're right," George started. "Our first introduction should have been better. I appreciate you calling me out on it. What about this? I'm going to give you my card and when you're ready, we'll have that cup of coffee."

George reached into his pocket, pulled out a business card, and extended it to DeMarcus. DeMarcus looked at it, then looked at George.

"Look as much as I appreciate the gesture and the fact you know me: why exactly do I need your business card or, with all due respect, your cup of coffee?"

George paused to look at him again. "Candid. I like it," he thought to himself.

"Well, your mom said you used to have an interest in the technology sector. I'm not sure if that's still the case. If it is, my company has a lot of connections and can help with that." George held back out that card.

With renewed interest, DeMarcus looked at the card then at George. He took it.

"What's the name of your company?"

"FutureTech. I'm the chief technology officer."

"FutureTech? Wait, isn't that one of the fastest-growing startups right now??" DeMarcus asked, startled. "They have a nearly billion dollar market cap."

"It's $1.5 billion as of yesterday with the new round of investment," George corrected.

"And YOU'RE the CTO??"

"Why do you sound so shocked?" George asked.

"I mean I thought CTO's were..." DeMarcus was trying to find the right way to phrase it.

"'Younger.'" George interjected. "Not so seasoned. That's what you were trying to say, right?"

"Maybe." DeMarcus looked at the card in his hand. He read it aloud, "George James...Chief Technology Officer."

"Look. If you're interested in that coffee, DeMarcus...let me know and we'll set it up. Alright, take care." With that, George turned around and walked off, nodding to the cashier as he left.

DeMarcus looked at George as he walked off then at his card. He wasn't sure what this meant. What it would lead to. He wasn't even sure if he wanted what it would lead to. The only thing he knew right now was that he needed answers, and it would have to start with the person who made the surprise introduction.

Chapter 4 - Confrontation

Delores always seemed to have a song on her heart. Either she was singing a hymn or some new Christian song. And she always loved to have some background noise: when she was home, either the TV turned to TBN or the news, or some Gospel music channel.

Maybe it was to drown out the background noise of Brownsville.

The two bedroom apartment that she and DeMarcus shared was quaint and she did everything to make it feel like home. Granted she always had a dream of living in a bigger home in Long Island, especially one with a garden. She had a budding green thumb and wanted to be able to express that in her OWN garden, far from the concrete of Brooklyn. It was a dream she had with Marcus.

And even though there was no evidence of such a home...ever being the woman of faith, she continued to thank Dad for it.

She always seemed to be thanking God for something: life, health, strength, answered prayers, unanswered prayers, and everything in between. Honestly, sometimes she felt like a fool. Why was she thanking Dad when everything seemed to crumble around her? How could she thank Dad with the death of her husband? How could she thank Dad when sometimes there were more bills than money? How could she continually thank Him when her own son seemed to be straying away from Him and SHE had no way to reach him? How could she continue to thank Him when the home she lived in was not the home she wanted?

But despite her doubts, she continued to press on in faith and give glory to Dad.

She heard the door behind her. “Hey ma,” DeMarcus said as he entered the apartment.

“Hey baby,” she said looking at him. “How was your day?”

“Interesting,” DeMarcus said. “But I’m sure you already knew that. I met a ‘George.’”

“Ahhhh…how did that go?” Delores asked, interested.

“Ma…why did you set that up? This guy bum-rushed me in the bookstore. I thought it was a joke for a minute.”

“Seriously DeMarcus,” Delores looked at her son with disbelief. “He ‘bum rushed’ you? Did he tackle you in the aisle? Did he spill some books on the floor? Did you call the police after?”

“You know what I mean,” DeMarcus said with a soft glare. “I just didn’t expect that and I wish I had some heads up.”

“Well, you’re not really a fan of meeting new people anymore. And knowing you, you would have accused me of meddling…”

“…which I am,” DeMarcus interjected.

“Boyyyy…” Delores said with the tone of “boy don’t play with me.” “Anyway…I think that George is the kind of man you need to spend more time with. You seem a little off since dad died. I honestly can’t pinpoint it.”

“What do you mean ‘off’? I go to church, have a job, and stay out of trouble. We both know how hard this is, especially in this neighborhood. I don't understand what you mean by 'off?'"

"Baby," Delores measured her words carefully and silently prayed for wisdom. "Yes: you do go to church, you do have a job, and you do stay out of trouble, but you haven't really been active in the church for quite some time. I mean, what friends do you really have at the church? And what groups are you a part of? This is not to say that 'activity' is the only measure of success in the church. But it's hard to grow cold when you're staying near the fire.

"And yes you do have a job," she continued. "But baby, that bookstore job is really for teenagers and kids on summer break. It's not a career. And it's not something that's going to lead to something greater.

"And yes you DO stay out of trouble. Dad knows I'm grateful to Him for that. But baby you don't seem to be going anywhere or really WANT to go anywhere. And baby we don't have to have much, but we DO have to have a desire for better. A desire for more."

He stood there quietly and took in everything she said. "Look ma," he said slowly. "I appreciate you, but I'm living the best I know how. I'm in the church, I read my bible, and I'm doing my best to keep 'unspotted from the world.' [1] And..." his phone went off. He looked at it briefly, it was a text from Ebony:

"Hey sexy. WYD later?"

"...living for God." he continued

Delores looked at her son. She realized the frontal attack wasn't going to work. She considered it help; he considered it nagging. And the truth is, no man (young or old) is positively changed by a woman's nagging. She had to change course.

"Ok, no problem baby," she said. "But I do think George is an incredible resource for you to get into the tech sector. He is a strong man of God, a good family man, and he is successful. I thank Dad that your father and I knew him for so many years."

"So who is he?" DeMarcus asked.

"Well, what most people don't know is that George is one of the founders of FutureTech. He started the company over 20 years ago.

"Wait, what???" DeMarcus said shocked.

"George really is not into being a high profile. He always said that sometimes being in the light brought unnecessary heat. So once the company started to find its footing he took the CTO position. He still helps in making critical decisions for the business but it's not as prominent as the CEO position. And he is working to transition out of the business entirely.

"Why?" DeMarcus asked.

"He and his wife Candice have always had a heart for missionary work. They wanted to help others, but George said he never wanted to worry about money while doing that. So their plan was to build a business, make it successful, and transition out. He seems to be right on track."

"Wow. So he's nothing to play with." DeMarcus chuckled. "But wait, why have I never heard of him till today?"

"Baby, most people in the church don't even know that George is a multi-millionaire...probably a billionaire soon.

He rarely gives interviews, stays out of the limelight, and doesn't flaunt his wealth. For all people know, he's just a nice guy with a good job."

"Soooo...how do we know about him?" DeMarcus asked.

"Everyone loved your father. And George was no exception. George loved Marcus' influential nature and Marcus loved George's drive. They were really getting to know one another until..." her voice trailed off.

"...until dad died." DeMarcus said.

It took a minute for Delores to compose herself as the memories of her husband seemed to crash in all at once. "Yes, baby...until your dad died," she said. "That's why I think that George is a resource you SHOULD use. You used to have this desire to be in the tech industry...to be more. Now you just seem to be...." She looked for the right word. "Coasting."

DeMarcus turned away from his mom and thought about what she said. He knew she always had his best interest in mind. She was right. His life seemed to be on neutral. He used to have so much desire, so much fervor. He was even involved in the church more. There's no way he would've had time for an Ebony or all the other things that seem to be taking his time. He used to talk to his dad about all these dreams and ambitions; he still remembered the reassurance when his dad would pray for him and "bless" him.

He just couldn't understand why mom's "Dad" killed his dad.

"DeMarcus," Delores started softly. "Please say something."

"I'll look into George. There's nothing wrong with having people know you. I'm just gonna go to bed ma. I already ate and I'm pretty tired."

He was thinking about doing some research on George...and answering Ebony's text.

"Ok baby I love you."

"Love you too ma."

Chapter 5 - The Great Confession

It was 9 am when DeMarcus left to go to the bookstore. After some flirty conversation with Ebony and a plan to meet later on, he did his research on George. There really wasn't much. He was a black man at the helm of one of the fastest-growing tech firms in North America. At first, he thought his mother was mistaken - there was nothing that said he was the founder of the firm. Not even on the company's website.

It wasn't until he did some further digging that he indeed verified it: he was one of the company co-founders. "Why wouldn't he stay in that role?" he thought to himself. "It's probably the first question I should ask him," he chuckled to himself.

After his research, DeMarcus reached out to George. He emailed him and was expecting a response maybe a day or two later...but was shocked to get a response a few minutes later. They decided to meet after his shift.

He was going to meet Ebony at 8 pm and since his shift ended at 5 pm he felt that was enough time. He started to feel that familiar guilt. He knew what meeting her led to--even though he swore that the last time would be the last time.

There was a common saying in the church: "hold unto God." The more he thought about his indiscretions, he realized how faulty the saying was. Because even though he found himself pulling away from God, even though he was in Ebony's bed more than he could count, and even though he was not living a life "on purpose" he could feel God still trying to help him. Trying to put him back on the right path.

He realized the truth: ***we don't hold unto God, He holds unto us.***

The day finally ended, and he was ready to meet George. Questions swirled through his mind:

Why would this undercover multi-millionaire want to meet him? What were they going to talk about? Stocks? Bonds? Futures? Was he going to offer him a job?

If he did, what would DeMarcus bring to the table?

All these and other questions swirled in his mind as he approached the coffee shop where he and George agreed to meet. As he walked in, he saw George reading a Tablet. He seemed deeply mired in thought. What was he reading? A prospectus that outlined his company's IPO? A business article? Funny cat videos?

"That looks like a pretty interesting read," DeMarcus started walking to the table. "What is that? 'The Journal?' 'Businessweek'?" He sat down.

"Nah," George looked up with those intense eyes. "I read that already. This is more interesting to me right now." George turned around the tablet and DeMarcus saw he was reading the Book of Proverbs.

"Oh!" DeMarcus said.

"Why so surprised?" George asked.

"I figured an 'important' guy like you would be reading some business stuff...or watching cat videos...whatever appeals to you," DeMarcus said.

George chuckled. "I'm not sure who the 'important' person you're talking about is. And maybe I watched the cat videos before you got here. But there's a lot of 'business stuff' right here."

"I'm not sure what Business stuff you're talking about," DeMarcus said.

"I'll tell you a story," George said as he put down the tablet. "There was a guy named Steve Scott who flunked out of his first six jobs after college."

"Wait...six!" DeMarcus said.

"Yup. Six. Some he was fired from, some he quit, and some he quit before he got fired. After the sixth job loss, he went to one of his best friends, perplexed. He said, 'I don't understand--no matter what I do, no matter how hard I work, I just can't succeed.' His friend didn't give him any advice that moment, he just went home and prayed about it. The next morning his friend came back and gave him an answer. He told Scott to read a chapter of Proverbs every morning for two years, write down the insight learned, and apply them to work."

"Okaaayyyy?" DeMarcus asked wondering where this was going.

"So," George continued. "He did it. Now I'm not going to tell you that things immediately shifted. He lost his seventh and eighth job. But on the NINTH, he created a television marketing campaign that DOUBLED the company's sales in only four months."

"Whoa! Nice," DeMarcus said. "So was he promoted? Given a company car?"

"Funny you say that," George said. "They offered him, vice president of marketing, WITH a company car."

"See I was right," DeMarcus said with a chuckle. "So he took the position, moved up to CEO, and became rich. The end."

"Not quite. He actually turned it down and quit soon after."

"Wait what?!"

"Yup."

"Uh...this story kind of sucks."

"It wouldn't if you let me finish," George looked at him with slight annoyance.

DeMarcus quickly shut up.

"Anyway. He turned it down so he could start his own marketing company. Within nine months, their sales had grown to nearly one million dollars a week."

DeMarcus sat there in silence.

"This guy," George continued. "Went on to build a dozen companies from scratch achieving over a billion dollars in sales. So...there's a lot of insight and business knowledge in this Book." He said this while lifting up his tablet. "It's NOT just about getting you to heaven. But that's another lesson for another time."

"Lesson?" DeMarcus asked. "What lesson are you trying to teach me?"

"All of life is a lesson DeMarcus IF we're willing to learn," George said. "But regarding you, I don't know if I can teach you anything. People who learn something want to be taught something. I don't think you're at the stage where you want to learn from me. But, your mother DID ask me to talk to you…"

"Concerning my coasting life?" DeMarcus interjected with slight sarcasm.

"About where she sees you going," George responded, ignoring his sarcasm. "About the fact that we ALL get stuck at times."

DeMarcus wasn't fully ready to have this conversation. So he turned the conversation into something more interesting. "Is it true you started the company? And is it true, it's going public soon?" He said.

"Regarding the first question: yes. Regarding the second: I will neither confirm nor deny," George said with a smile.

"So what's your story? Where are you from? Why THIS business? And why did you step down from running it?" DeMarcus wanted to know everything.

George held up his hand. "Whoa…whoa…whoa. All that will be answered in time IF we continue."

"What do you mean 'if'" DeMarcus asked.

"Well you probably don't know this, but I lead a very busy life with my family and my company. Those things matter to me the most. And as much as I don't want to waste your time. I definitely am not going to waste mine. And if I feel that meeting with you is a waste of my time--as much I respect your mother--I have no problem in shaking hands and parting as friends."

The comment sat in the air for a minute. It brought DeMarcus back to earth. Originally, in the back of his mind, he thought he was helping his mom by meeting George. But now, as he thought about it: this guy was an accomplished multi-millionaire taking time to talk to him.

"Ok," DeMarcus said slowly. "I can respect that. I'm not above learning. And obviously, there are some things you can teach me. What do you feel has been one of the most effective lessons for you?"

"Hold that thought. Let's grab some coffee. What do you want? My treat."

After getting some drinks and pastries, George sat back down with DeMarcus.

"To answer your last question, I'll tell you a story..." George started.

"Hmm, he IS a big 'story' man," DeMarcus thought to himself.

"...there was a farmer by the name of Charles Capps. He sold a farm and invested the proceeds into a business. The business flopped and he lost his original investment plus $25,000 more. This was in the '60s so you can only imagine what that would be today. He was deeply in debt, frustrated, AND was a Christian. For years all he would do is confess how bad things were, how they weren't going to change, etc. Needless to say, things got worse. He borrowed $100,000 to pay his back bills. He went to church but got nothing from the sermons. All he could think about was his money or lack thereof."

"Wow, that sucks," DeMarcus said.

"Yes, it does...or did. So anyway, he got some material that talked about the power of speaking God's Word. He read it and other material like it. Soon because he was more in the Word, God began to speak to him. See DeMarcus everyone wants to hear God, but very few want to read His Word. But the best way to hear Him is through His Word."

DeMarcus thought about that for a second. Then he thought about his mom. She always said she learned more about "Dad" from His love letters (or her Bible).

"According to Capps," George continued. "God told him to search for promises related to his situation, write them down, and speak them aloud. Doing that would build his faith. So he did it, and found Promises related to abundance and prosperity. He did it for nearly a year and within that time, he paid off his debts and went on to become a Bible teacher teaching what he'd learned."

"Whoa...okay," DeMarcus said. "So you're saying that he started speaking prosperity Scriptures and a duffle bag full of money came out of heaven?" DeMarcus asked with a grin.

"Not quite," George said with a smile. "He did it for a while, felt like a fraud, kept doing it, and started to see himself as abundant even when he was still broke. Then he got the idea to buy some land, somehow found financing to develop it, and sold it for a hefty profit. Since then, he was a real estate developer AND Bible teacher. So no, there was no duffle bag full of money."

"Wait, wait?? You said he was already in debt so how could he get financing? Didn't they check his credit? His debt to income ratio?" DeMarcus asked.

"I agree with you. If someone was in debt up to their gills like that it'd be hard for them to get the extra financing. I'm not even sure that would work today, to be honest. But, according to him, God told him to do it, and it worked out."

"So you're saying," DeMarcus started. "That the secret to success...even your success was declaring Bible Scriptures?"

George thought about the question for a minute.

"I'll say this: there is power in what you say...especially as a believer," George said. "From a psychological standpoint, we're all like computers. In computer programming, a script is a program or list of commands. The computer doesn't do what it wants to do; in essence, it's bound by its list of commands or its script. We're the same way: we have limitless potential but we are bound by OUR scripts. If our scripts - or internal programming - is good, we can do some amazing things. But if it's bad, no matter how much potential we have, we'll be limited by it."

"What do you mean?" DeMarcus asked with interest.

"Hmmm...have you ever seen a beautiful girl with low self-esteem?"

"All the time."

"To you: she's amazing. But to her: she doesn't measure up. And whether it was through some traumatic event or poor family upbringing, her script is subpar."

"Mmmmmmm."

"I know. Now to be honest, we all have some poor programming, but this is why God works so hard in reprogramming us. And He does that with His Scripts...*or Script-ures*. He puts out those Script-ures, but it is our responsibility to rescript or reprogram ourselves."

"And you're saying the only way to do that is by saying it?" DeMarcus asked.

“Well, let me ask you: if someone goes around always calling themselves ‘stupid’ will they get smarter over time? No. They’ll progressively get worse. Or will someone who rehearses everything they can’t do reach high levels of achievement? Probably not. The truth is this: over time, you see what you say.”

“That’s deep,” DeMarcus said. An appreciation for George and his insight was starting to grow. He was a perfect combination of spiritual and practical application.

“So if what we tell ourselves is important, how much more important is it when we tell it with the Word of God?” George continued. “How powerful it is when we rescript ourselves saying: ‘I’m blessed,’ ‘I’m highly favored,’ ‘I’m the head,’ ‘I’m not the tail,’ ‘I’m above only and not beneath,’ ‘ I’m accepted in the beloved’ ‘Whatever I do prospers?’ I know for me, when I started declaring God’s Promises for abundance, nothing immediately happened. I kept doing it and soon got the idea for my company. I kept doing it and found some good partners. I kept doing it in the beginning when things were really rough. I also did it when no money was coming in and I felt like a fool. But God really does watch over His Word [1] and over time, things began to change.”

“Hold up, does this help in any other way besides just making money?” DeMarcus asked. “Not to say money isn’t important but does this have broader applications?”

“Good question,” George said. “Let’s say it like this: most people try to change their lives from outcomes, but the best way to do it is from identity. For example, if two people were offered cigarettes, one person might say ‘No thanks, I am trying to quit.’ Whereas the other person might say ‘No thanks, I’m not a smoker.’ That second person is speaking from the concept of who they are, while the first is speaking from the concept of what they do."

"I don't understand," DeMarcus said.

"The most effective way to change your life is from a new identity. Because results will flow from that identity; let's say as a Christian man, I have a problem with lust. I could try to change from actions: not doing lustful deeds. Or, I could change from identity: realizing I am the righteousness of God. If I am the righteousness of God I realize lust doesn't fit in with my identity--holiness does. And I will do those deeds that represent holiness."

DeMarcus was a little startled. George was speaking to the very thing he was dealing with and he was right. Did Mom tell him to say this? DeMarcus didn't see himself as "holy" he saw himself as "trying to be right." And as much as he tried, he was failing.

"Jesus said it like this," George continued oblivious to DeMarcus' internal battle. "'I am the vine; you are the branches. If you remain in Me and I in you, you will bear much fruit; apart from Me, you can do nothing.'[2] A fruitful tree doesn't try to produce fruit. It just does. Because that's what it is. The same thing with a fruitful person: they are going to produce no matter what. A winner will always win. And unfortunately, a loser will always find ways to lose."

"But wait, aren't we graded on our results? Does 'being' pay bills?" DeMarcus said with a chuckle.

George looked at his potential new mentee for a second. He was insightful and asked smart questions. "He DOES have a lot of possibilities," George thought to himself.

"You're correct, 'being' by itself doesn't pay bills," George started. "But 'being' produces doing. If someone is a born-again Christian, what is something they're going to do that's in line with their identity?"

"Read their Bible...pray...go to church..." DeMarcus started.

"Exactly! Their sustained actions will proceed from their deeply held identity and beliefs. We all know people who do the 'right thing' for a while but because of how they view themselves they don't keep it up. In other words: someone who sees themself as a failure will not and cannot continue with successful deeds. And vice versa: a person who sees themself as successful can't help but do the things that make them successful."

"And that's why we 'rescript' ourselves?" DeMarcus asked, finally catching on.

"Yes. When we declare God's Word continually, it changes the way we view ourselves, it renews faith, and it helps in understanding His perfect Will for our lives."

DeMarcus sat there for a while--processing all the advice he just heard. He realized that George was on a different plane of spirituality than he was. He saw the Bible as an outdated rule book, but George viewed it as a Guidebook for life. DeMarcus thought about his walk with God: it didn't have the same vitality and practicality. His salt had lost its savor. He then looked at his phone and realized his "appointment" with Ebony was coming up. DeMarcus was so conflicted. He wanted to be worthy of his call, but at the same time, he had needs; or urges. He needed advice so he decided to put his new mentor to the test.

“Want to ask you a question,” DeMarcus started. “Let’s say someone is struggling with lust; how should they handle it?”

George looked at DeMarcus straight in the eye. “Was he talking about himself or someone he knew?” he thought to himself, but he decided not to probe.

“Well, I know for me there are two main Scriptures that help me. The first one is in the book of Job.” George picked up his tablet and began scrolling. He finally got to Job 31. “This Scripture has really helped me over the years: ‘I made a covenant with my eyes not to look lustfully at a young woman.’[3] Whenever I get tempted to lust after an attractive woman this is what I say over and over in my head. And for someone who is struggling with lust, this other one helps immensely.”

George began to scroll through his tablet, found the Scripture he was looking for and gave the tablet to DeMarcus. DeMarcus looked at it and began to read.

“For this is the will of God, even your sanctification, that ye should abstain from fornication: That every one of you should know how to possess his vessel in sanctification and honour.” [4]

“I feel like the King James translation gives it the most meaning,” George interjected.

DeMarcus stared at the tablet for a while. There it was: the direct command from God to cease from sexual immorality and live a holy life. He decided to look at another translation and was shocked by what he further read:

“The Lord will punish all those who commit such sins, as we told you and warned you before. For God did not call us to be impure but to live a holy life. Therefore, anyone who rejects this instruction does not reject a human being but God, the very God who gives you his Holy Spirit." [5]

It was like a bomb went off: God didn't call him to Ebony's bed, He didn't call him into this impure lifestyle. As good as He was, God was not to be trifled with.

"Yeah," DeMarcus started. "I could see how these Scriptures could help. I'll...uh...pass them along."

George looked at DeMarcus for a second. It WAS for him. He could also see that God was dealing with him. He left it alone. Besides, the Holy Spirit was better at conviction than he was.

Also, he had to go.

"DeMarcus," George started. "I'm going to leave you those two Scriptures as an example. Again: what I would do is repeat them over and over. That's what the Bible calls confession. As I do that, I find that I will have the strength to overcome these sins. But here's what I'm also going to recommend for you: find, write down, and confess ten Scriptures related to success, abundance, and prosperity.[6]

Confess them over and over. Keep doing it even if it feels like nothing's working. That is your homework. But I do have to go. It's already late. When you're ready let's set up another time to meet-- probably at my office. Take care, DeMarcus."

And just like that, he left.

DeMarcus sat there for a while just replaying the events of what just happened with George. It was at that moment he realized: something needed to change. HE needed to change.

He looked over the two Scriptures George left - especially the one in 1st Thessalonians

"For this is the will of God, even your sanctification, that ye should abstain from fornication...

...for this is the will of God, even your sanctification, that ye should abstain from fornication...

...for this is the will of God, even your sanctification, that ye should abstain from fornication."

As he repeated it to himself, he was beginning to see the "trap" of his Ebony appointment. He had to put a stop to it. "...will of God...abstain from fornication." The more he said it, the more real it became.

He looked at his phone, found Ebony's number, texted her, and told her he couldn't make it after all, and they would have to reschedule. He put the phone in his pocket. He DID want to see her, but he knew he just made a significant step in his growth. Maybe there was something to be said of his meetings with George.

Chapter 6 - Generosity

A week had passed and DeMarcus had another meeting set up with George--this time in his office at FutureTech headquarters. Even though the urges were strong and he missed her, DeMarcus hadn't seen Ebony once that week. They texted back and forth, she flirted with him, he flirted with her, but the command to "abstain" held him in place. But to be honest, it wasn't just the command, it was him confessing the command. The more he confessed the Scriptures, the more they seemed to take on new life.

It seemed like his new mentor was onto something. DeMarcus also spent the week combing, Googling, and finding Scriptures on success. He found ten and added ten more. He confessed them in the morning and in the evening. He wanted the "good success" that was promised. [1]

After a while, he came to this conclusion: God was interested in his complete success. Not just material but relational, spiritual, physical, and etc. It seemed that God was intent on DeMarcus living his best life in Him.

He had so many more questions and couldn't wait to ask George. DeMarcus walked up to FutureTech's headquarters; He went to security and said his name and who he was there to see. The security guard gave him a slight look of disbelief but then asked for his ID. After calling up and getting the ok, he gave the ID back to DeMarcus and told him to go to the 22nd floor.

When he left the security desk, a realization hit him: George was largely responsible for the growth and success of this organization. Wow!

An assistant met him at the elevator on the 22nd floor. That assistant led him to George's office. DeMarcus was in awe when he saw the inside of the building - it was a mix of futuristic and minimalistic.

There were white computers everywhere, and it almost seemed like a sci-fi movie.

When they finally made it to George's office, the assistant smiled and then left. George sat behind a big white desk with two computer screens. He was finishing up some tasks and did not give much attention to DeMarcus. DeMarcus sat there patiently as George finished up, and with one final click of his keypad, he turned his energies toward DeMarcus.

"Hey, DeMarcus," George began. "Thanks for your patience. Hungry?"

"Starving," DeMarcus said.

"Ok. Let's grab some food in the cafeteria downstairs and bring it back here."

"Whatever you were working on looked really important. What was it?"

"Hmmm...we'll discuss it over lunch," George said.

As they walked from George's office to the cafeteria, George listened attentively as DeMarcus shared his progress: the Scriptures he had found and the confessions he had made. He didn't share anything about Ebony though. He respected George; he just didn't trust him that much yet.

They got their food and went back to George's office. George decided to share what he was working on.

"DeMarcus, if you had to guess who would you say was the richest Christian?" George asked.

"I don't know. You?" he asked with a chuckle

"No. I'm serious." George said with a grin. "And I appreciate the compliment. Who do you think was the richest Christian?"

"I don't know. David? Solomon?" DeMarcus guessed.

"Good guesses. I should have been more specific. This person was a non-biblical figure."

"I really don't know."

"It was John D. Rockefeller."

"Wait...what? Wasn't he like some kind of 'robber baron'? How do you know he was a Christian?"

"It's well documented that he was baptized, an active church member, and professed Christ as Lord."

"Well, how do we know that makes him a Christian?" DeMarcus asked skeptically

"Well, you've been baptized, you're an active church member, and profess Christ as Lord; how do we know that you're a Christian? Or that I'm a Christian? Or is anyone who does these things a Christian? We really don't."

"I see your point," DeMarcus said thoughtfully. "I guess the only person who would know if a person is a 'Christian' or not would be God."

"Right. But having studied Rockefeller's history and biography I do believe he was a Christian. And by many accounts, he was the richest American ever. At one point, his personal wealth was 1.5% to 2% of the U.S.'s GDP."

"Yeah...that's pretty rich!"

"He had many business holdings and actually made more in his retirement than in his working days. But that's not the lesson I want to share with you today. Remember when you asked what important thing I was working on before we came here?"

"Yeah. What was it? A new product? Some cutting-edge software? Email?"

"Not quite. I was paying my tithes and donating money toward some important causes."

"Wait...what? That's the important thing you were doing and the 'lesson' you want to teach me?"

"Yes. The reason I brought up Rockefeller was that he learned to give at a very early age. He started out giving 6% of his earnings to charity. By the time he was twenty, his giving had exceeded 10% of his income; much of it going to church-related activities. He believed that his success was divinely inspired. He himself said: 'God gave me my money.'

"In fact, in his seventies, he believed that his giving was the reason for his success. He said and I quote: 'It had seemed as if I was favored and got increase because the Lord knew I was going to turn it around and give it back.'"

"Hmmm, that's a very nice lesson from Rockefeller. And I'm sure there are some lessons in his giving. But I find it hard to believe that tithing is the main reason for him being the richest man in the world," DeMarcus said flatly.

"Why?" George asked.

"I mean," DeMarcus started. "Aren't there people that tithe and give to the church and hardly have anything to show for it? AND this sounds like something the church would be preaching if they needed money for the building fund."

They both shared a laugh as they realized the irony.

"While you're right that there are churches and organizations that 'sell' tithing for selfish means...and there are people that haven't seen the true benefit of it. You shouldn't write it off. In fact, in Jewish culture, tithing is considered an ancient formula for becoming wealthy. In their Talmud, it says: 'Tithe so that you will become rich.'" [2]

"Really?"

"Yup. Tithing in Jewish culture is considered a partnership between the giver and God. The giver partners with God in helping the world. God partners with the giver in business affairs. In the church, it is more ridiculed and scrutinized. But again: that's because people don't really understand the power of it. And yes, it doesn't make logical sense to give away money, especially when we need money."

"It makes absolutely no sense. If I'm struggling, why would I give away the very thing I need?"

George looked at DeMarcus for a second. Rather than respond, he opened his phone, went to his Bible app, and carefully searched for a Scripture. "DeMarcus read this for me," George said, handing DeMarcus his phone.

DeMarcus took the phone and read, "There is one who scatters, yet increases more, and there is one who withholds more than is right. But it leads to poverty." [3]

"What do you think that means?"

"I honestly have no idea."

"In God's system, to give more is to gain more. The more love we give to others, the more love we receive; the more praise and gratitude we give Him, the more He intercedes; and the more money we give the more He gives back to us. In God's Kingdom: to give up is to go up."

DeMarcus thought the last thing George said: "to give up is to go up." It lingered in his head for a minute. It had so many practical applications. Or did it?

"Let me ask you this," DeMarcus started. "Are there any practical applications to this tithing/giving thing?"

George looked at DeMarcus, then looked to the left, then to the right, and then said with a chuckle "You mean, besides me?"

"Yeah. I don't hear them talking about tithing/giving in Forbes, Fortune, Businessweek, or the Journal." He said this as if he was a regular reader.

"Hmmm...I'll tell you a story. Have you ever heard of R.G. LeTourneau?"

"No."

"Well, he was an industrialist who created earthmoving machines. When he got into business, he decided to make God his partner. As the business struggled and grew, he prioritized donating money to certain missions. One year he made the decision to not give that money away but to invest it back in the business. His reasoning was that if he invested in the business the next year, he'd be able to give God that offering and more."

"I can see the reasoning," DeMarcus nodded.

"Well, the next year the business suffered a major setback. They almost went under. He realized his error and started donating again. The next year he saw a profit. In fact, hold on. I read his autobiography and have a picture of a page in the book. I keep it with me as a reminder when I feel like I want to withhold. Here it is:"

George pulled out his phone and started to read the picture of a page.

"'Just to give you an idea, the year I failed to share with the Lord, my profits were, as mentioned, $34,474.92. The next year of 1931, I had almost the same figure - $32,507.41 - as a loss, and the worst was yet to come. By mid-1932 I had sunk $100,000 below bottom, but had recognized my error and was back in the good graces of my Lord. We ended that year with a net profit of $52,055.61, meaning we had earned that much even if we did owe it all and then some. But with substantial payments on our debts, Frost was able to re-establish our credit rating, and while we were still living hand-to-mouth, we did have beans in the pantry.'" [4]

"Wow. That's crazy! Two questions: who was Frost? And how did he get out of all the debt he was in?"

"There was a surety company that backed LeTourneau on a construction job when he posted that $100,000 loss. Keep in mind again DeMarcus, this was in the '30s...that's a LOT of money. So the surety company was going to make sure they paid them back every penny owed."

"Sure-ty company," DeMarcus asked puzzled.

"'Surety' means the guarantee of the debts of one party by another. So if I borrow money from another person and you're the surety company you're going to guarantee that debt in the event I default. This is done if my credit or credibility is in question. Got it?"

"Yup."

"So the surety company who wanted to make sure they got paid sent in an accountant by the name of Mr. Frost. Mr. Frost was to fix the books. To answer your second question, LeTourneau changed the way he did business. At the time his business model was a contractor using his machines on the job. As a contractor, he was always looking for work--it was always up and down. While doing contracting work, he was selling earth-moving machines on the side. His lawyer hinted at the idea of solving his financial woes by going full force into the manufacturing business rather than rolling the dice on the ups and downs of big construction jobs. And the rest is history."

"Wow. Soooo...is that a giving lesson or a business lesson?"

George thought about it for a minute. "I guess you could say both. The giving lesson is that you can do more giving to God than withholding from Him. The business lesson is that real wealth is NOT built on your physical labor but on products or services that don't always require the sweat of your brow."

DeMarcus sat there processing everything George said: the tithe, the story, the lesson after, etc. It sounded good, but he still wasn't that convinced.

"Let's play devil's advocate. That's great about Rockefeller, LeTourneau, and yourself, but there are people who do tithe and have nothing to show for it. What about them?"

“Good question. Truth is: it’s not about tithes...it’s about tithes AND offerings. It is the amount that is given above the tithes that matter.”

“What do you mean?”

“DeMarcus I’m not going to go into the Biblical debate about whether tithing is for new testament believers or whether it was just for people under the law. That debate is never going to go away. I believe in tithing, but I equally believe in offerings. I believe the power for exponential increase begins when we give over the tithe. The tithe is what we give back to God. It’s His. The offering is what we voluntarily give to Him. And it’s also with the attitude in which we give it.”

George started looking through his phone again. Obviously, he was looking for something for DeMarcus to read as that was now his custom. He handed the phone to DeMarcus. “Read this.” DeMarcus took the phone, looked at the highlighted passage, and read,

“Remember this, he who sows sparingly and grudgingly will also reap sparingly and grudgingly, and he who sows generously [that blessings may come to someone] will also reap generously and with blessings.

“Let each one [give] as he has made up his own mind and purposed in his heart, not reluctantly or sorrowfully or under compulsion, for God loves (He takes pleasure in, prizes above other things, and is unwilling to abandon or to do without) a cheerful (joyous, ‘prompt to do it’) giver [whose heart is in his giving].

“And God is able to make all grace (every favor and earthly blessing) come to you in abundance, so that you may always and under all circumstances and whatever the need be self-sufficient [possessing enough to require no aid or support and furnished in abundance for every good work and charitable donation].

"As it is written, He [the benevolent person] scatters abroad; He gives to the poor; His deeds of justice and goodness and kindness and benevolence will go on and endure forever!

"And [God] Who provides seed for the sower and bread for eating will also provide and multiply your [resources for] sowing and increase the fruits of your righteousness [which manifests itself in active goodness, kindness, and charity].

"Thus you will be enriched in all things and in every way so that you can be generous, and [your generosity as it is] administered by us will bring forth thanksgiving to God." [5]

"A lot huh?" George asked with a chuckle.

"You sure love different versions, don't you?" DeMarcus said with a grin.

"When I grew up in the church, it was always 'King James.' But as I grew in my relationship with God, I realized some versions help express the ideas more clearly. The King James version was originally created to make the Bible more palatable to everyday people. So because of the Greek meaning of some words, sometimes one version doesn't get the entire meaning. That's why I like the different versions to get different perspectives of what God is saying."

"Almost like the Gospels?" DeMarcus said.

"What do you mean?"

"Well the Gospels technically were written by four men," DeMarcus started. "Each had their own perspective on the life of Jesus. I guess there never is just one way to look at what God is doing. He's multifaceted and our way of viewing Him has to be multifaceted."

George stared at DeMarcus for a second. He was insightful, spoke his truth, and had a stronger Biblical foundation than he (George) originally thought.

"Yes, you're right." George started. "Absolutely right. So that's my reasoning for the different versions. But as it relates to giving--I believe--in order for it to be effective, it has to be above the tithe."

"And done with a certain 'attitude?'"

"Yes!"

"What do you mean by that?"

"Well let's say you decided to buy a dozen roses for your future wife. You wrap it up nicely and it looks presentable. You go home and hand it to her and just say 'here!' Just by your attitude, she probably won't accept it. Even if it looks nice and it's the 'right' thing to do, it'll be a no-go. Let's say you do it again, but this time you say, 'Babe I'm grateful for who you are and what you do. You mean the world to me and this is just a token of that appreciation.' Which one is she going to accept?"

"Probably the second one," DeMarcus said.

"Why?"

"Because of the way I gave it and the attitude in which I gave it."

"Exactly. And if your earthly wife feels like that, what makes you think your Heavenly Father is any different?"

"Good point."

"DeMarcus, most people who do tithe do it under compulsion. And the Scripture you read just shows that God doesn't want that kind of giving. He loves the person whose heart is in their giving. He loves the person who does it with appreciation. Jesus actually modeled that kind of giving and increase."

"What do you mean?"

"You know the story of Jesus feeding the multitude with two small fishes and five loaves of bread, right?"

"Of course."

"When Jesus took that food which was not enough, He gave thanks for it and it became more than enough.[6]

When we make that sacrifice to give our tithes AND offerings and we do it with gratitude; gratitude for Who He is, what He has done, and what He is about to do, I believe that's when He goes to work multiplying our resources."

George looked briefly at his watch.

"I have a meeting at 1:15 I have to prepare for. So we have another few minutes. Ok?"

"That's fine. And I do appreciate the time you're spending with me. Just want to show you my gratitude," DeMarcus said with a grin.

They both shared a quick laugh.

"Well, I'm glad to see that you're getting it. But I want you not to miss this part. When I say God is going to multiply your resources, don't expect a check in the mail or a duffle bag full of money. I'm not saying there aren't miracles where

God impresses people to give money. They do happen. But to rely on these 'handouts' is not the way to His wealth. Are you familiar with Jeremiah 29:11?" [7]

"Vaguely."

"It says, 'For I know the plans I have for you, declares the LORD, plans to prosper you and not to harm you, plans to give you hope and a future.'"

"So we're just gonna quote random Scriptures from memory now, huh? So we're a theologian too?"

George smiled at DeMarcus' humor.

"Anyway," George said with a chuckle. "I believe that when we give our tithes and offerings in a way that honors Him, He then shows us His plans for our abundance. It's almost like the plans were already there from the beginning, but the sacrifice just unlocked them."

"Almost like a cheat code?" DeMarcus said.

"Yeah...almost like a cheat code. He shows us what to build, buy, do, or be in order to multiply our resources for sowing."

"Whoa! That's crazy!"

"DeMarcus, remember what Jesus said: 'Give, and it shall be given unto you; good measure, pressed down, and shaken together, and running over, shall men give into your bosom.'[8] Your wealth is going to come from other people giving into your 'bosom.' But those people are going to expect something in exchange for their money. This is where God comes in: He shows you a product or service you can give these people in exchange for their money. This at least has been my experience."

"George, you're speaking about entrepreneurs. What if I'm not called to be 'entrepreneurial?'"

"Well," George began while looking at his watch. "Consider what the word 'entrepreneur' actually means. The word is derived from an old French word that means 'manages or undertakes.' So anyone who undertakes, manages, and is responsible for some venture is technically an entrepreneur. An entrepreneur is not just a business owner, DeMarcus. Don't believe the hype. Anyone who is responsible for their career, finances, or success IS an entrepreneur. But...I do have to go. What did you learn today?"

DeMarcus thought for a second.

"There is power in giving," he started. "Giving involves tithes AND offerings. The attitude in which you give is as important as what you give. God loves a cheerful giver. And as we give, God helps us in multiplying our resources."

"Good. Good job. You learned a lot. Take care, DeMarcus."

And just like that, George turned back to his computer screens.

DeMarcus walked away thinking about everything George said. It was deep but so simple. He explained it in a way where he could see the spiritual and practical application. It just made sense. George's talks with him made him realize how much he didn't know...and how much he had to learn.

"Lord, help me to be the man You've called me to be," DeMarcus silently prayed.

Chapter 7 - Making the Cut

Delores stared at the bills.

How was she going to make it? The car note, credit cards, and hospital bills from Marcus' stay were due. "And my God shall supply all your needs according to His riches in glory by Christ Jesus"[1] kept ringing in her head. But right now she couldn't see it.

She didn't see it in her bank account.

She didn't see it with the city job she held for nearly 30 years. A job she was grateful for but wished she could retire from. She just didn't see it. And she couldn't see God in this.

She tithed and gave offerings and Dad took care of her--but she wanted more. She wanted to be debt-free; she wanted to not have to worry about money; she wanted more than her apartment in Brooklyn - she wanted her own home. She wanted to travel more.

"Dad," she prayed. "I need help. I don't know what to do. I look to You, but with Marcus gone these bills are piling up. You said You'd supply all my needs, but Daddy I don't see it right now. Nevertheless, I thank You for who You Are and what You are doing. Even though I don't see it."

She praised and thanked Him for an answer she couldn't see. And even though the bills were still present, she felt a weight lifted off her shoulders.

"Thank You for everything, Daddy. Thank You for hearing and answering me. You are my helper. I will not be afraid. You are still my Shepherd and I do not lack. You said that I would be abundantly satisfied with the fatness of Your House.[2] Thank you."

Suddenly a Scripture flashed in her mind. She couldn't quite remember it so she picked up her Bible. "It's somewhere in Matthew I think."

Suddenly she found it and just like that she knew everything was going to be alright. It read:

"Therefore I say to you, do not worry about your life, what you will eat or what you will drink; nor about your body, what you will put on. Is not life more than food and the body more than clothing? Look at the birds of the air, for they neither sow nor reap nor gather into barns; yet your heavenly Father feeds them. Are you not of more value than they? Which of you by worrying can add one cubit to his stature?

"So why do you worry about clothing? Consider the lilies of the field, how they grow: they neither toil nor spin; and yet I say to you that even Solomon in all his glory was not arrayed like one of these. Now if God so clothes the grass of the field, which today is, and tomorrow is thrown into the oven, will He not much more clothe you, O you of little faith?

"Therefore do not worry, saying, 'What shall we eat?' or 'What shall we drink?' or 'What shall we wear?' For after all these things the Gentiles seek. For your heavenly Father knows that you need all these things. But seek first the kingdom of God and His righteousness, and all these things shall be added to you. Therefore do not worry about tomorrow, for tomorrow will worry about its own things. Sufficient for the day is its own trouble." [3]

She put down her Bible and put away the bills for now. Somehow, someway she would be fine.

She began to think about all the good things God had done for her and suddenly, her mind ran on DeMarcus. She was seeing some differences in him since he began speaking with George. There was more purpose to step. When she went into his empty room she'd see his Bible open more. She even heard him whispering Scriptures under his breath.

At that moment she heard the door open.

"Evening Ma!"

"How are you doing baby? How was your day?"

"It was good. We both know how exciting it can be at the bookstore," DeMarcus said with a smile.

"Mmmm Hmmm. VERY exciting. How do you deal with all the stress?"

If there is one thing Delores was extremely grateful for was the bond she shared with her son. Considering her upbringing, she wondered how good a mother SHE would be. It was something she prayed earnestly about.

She prayed for the wisdom to nurture but not coddle; to be candid but not harsh; to speak the truth but to do it in love; to listen, empathize, and learn to respect him as a person. And even though their relationship was not perfect, she was grateful it was strong.

"You know ma I'm not gonna give you the satisfaction of saying that you might've been right," he said, not looking directly at her. "But...I will say that maybe it is time for me to start looking elsewhere."

Delores realized that it took a lot for a person to say when they were wrong. As much as she wanted to celebrate, she kept her composure and silently thanked Dad for the work He was doing behind the scenes.

"Ok. Well since I'm not getting any 'satisfaction' from that comment," she said with slight sarcasm. "What were you thinking? What job were you thinking about?"

"I don't know honestly. But I do think it is something back in technology. Just watching what George does in technology is really...wow! You know that was where I was headed...but when dad died..." His words just trailed off.

"I know, baby. When your dad went home, it threw us all for a loop. There's not a day I don't miss him. And the truth is: I still question Dad why he took him home so early."

"What you need to be questioning," DeMarcus thought to himself. "Is that why YOUR Dad did nothing to save my dad?" He knew saying it out loud would lead to conversations he wasn't ready to have.

"And also...I'm not going to give you the satisfaction of introducing me to George," DeMarcus said. "It definitely has NOT been a good experience. I haven't learned anything from him," he said with a chuckle.

"Mmmm hmmm," Delores said with a slight grin. "Well, what have you NOT been learning from George?" She said as she sat on the family couch.

"Honestly," he began while sitting in the armchair. "He's shared a lot. Mostly Bible stuff, but he shares it in a way that makes it really practical. He also LOVES telling stories. He's like a modern-day Dr. Seuss."

"That's good. So he's a good teacher?"

"Yeah. He does make it simple and digestible. I'm meeting with him tomorrow."

"That's good, baby. I'm glad to hear. I'm not cooking tonight baby, what do you want for dinner?"

"I guess Chinese. But whatever it is: it's on me. It's my way of NOT showing appreciation to a pretty wise lady," DeMarcus said with a smile.

Delores took a fake swipe at her son's head.

"Boy, if you don't get out of here and order us some food. Talking 'bout you NOT gonna show appreciation. You will appreciate and give me every rose while I'm alive and AFTER I go home to Daddy," she said with a laugh.

DeMarcus went to his room to grab the menu of their nearby Chinese restaurant. He truly was grateful for his mom, her wisdom, and their relationship. After she told him her order he looked at his phone and saw that he had a text message from Ebony.

A chill went down his spine. He hadn't seen or talked to her for two weeks. They would text now and then but it always ended when he turned down her invites. He clicked on the message:

"Hey stranger."

"Hey beautiful, how are you?" he responded.

"Are you busy?"

"No."

"I'm near your crib...can we meet and talk?"

He thought about it...

"Sure. Five minutes?"

"Cool."

He took that five minutes to go to the restroom, brush his teeth, wash his face, and order the food for pickup. His mind was racing with what he was going to tell her. His relationship with God had grown. It's not that He DIDN'T want her. He did. He was just tired of the guilt. He was tired of the endless loop: do it, feel guilty, promise to never do it again, get tempted, and end up doing it. Where would it end?

"Hey ma," DeMarcus said as he came back into the living room. "I'm gonna go pick up the food."

"You sure baby?" Delores asked from the kitchen. "Didn't you just come in? Why not have them deliver?"

"I feel like going for a walk. I'll be back."

DeMarcus began the trek outside: through the apartment door, the long hallway, and the outside door. He stood on the stoop for a second looking around and finally saw Ebony across the street. He almost forgot how beautiful she was: she stood there in her wheat nubuck boots, tight jeans, jacket, and NY baseball cap.

"Damn," he said to himself as he walked over.

"Hey stranger," she said.

"How you doing?" he responded. They hugged and kissed.

"I'm doing fine. The question is: 'how are you doing?' I was wondering how witness protection is."

He laughed. He knew what she meant. It was a term they used when they hadn't seen each other much.

"You know how it is, just staying out of the public eye."

"I see that."

“Wanna take a walk?” DeMarcus asked.

“Sure,” she said as they started off together. “DeMarcus, did I do something wrong?”

“No. You haven’t.”

“Then why have you been avoiding me? And please don’t tell me something like ‘I’ve been busy.’ What is it? Is it some other girl?”

“It’s not that,” DeMarcus started. “The truth is: I’ve been meeting with this dude...a strong Christian dude...and he’s been helping with my faith and stuff. Me getting closer to God has made me realize the things I should be doing...and the things I shouldn’t.”

“Mmm-hmm...and I’m guessing some of those ‘things’ include the things we do. Or the things you do to me,” She drew closer.

“Yes. Those things,” he said as he pulled back slightly.

“DeMarcus, I’m a religious person. And we both know God IS love. So how can the love we share be taking you away from God?”

Her logic made sense and for a moment it stopped him in his tracks. They both walked in silence as he collected his thoughts. The next thought he had made him grit his teeth. He knew it was the right thing to say but it hurt saying:

“Eb, what we have is sex. It’s not love. It’s an expression of love in marriage. But since we’re not married...” his voice trailed.

“So what you tryna to get married?” she snapped.

"No," he said sternly. "I'm trying to live for God. I can't do that in your bed."

"Look, DeMarcus, I'm not really looking for a boyfriend, husband, or anything like that right now. And I can have any dude I want...but I like what YOU do for me. Are you saying you want to stop all this for some church?"

He thought about it for a minute while walking. What Ebony offered to him was something he liked...loved. That he couldn't deny. But could he really continue this hypocrisy? Could he continue to put the Creator on hold for the thing he created?

"I'm not ending this for church...I'm ending this because of my commitment to Christ. And THAT holds more weight for me," he said.

The reality of what was said sucked the air out of the conversation. They reached the Chinese restaurant. Ebony looked DeMarcus in the eyes--she could see that he was serious.

"Ok DeMarcus," she began. "I don't think there is anything else for us to talk about. I wish you the best and hope you're happy with your decision."

With that, she was gone. DeMarcus watched her as she walked away. He knew he made the right decision, but he still felt regret. What is it about the end of a relationship that makes us remember the beginning? DeMarcus thought about how he met her, asked for her number, their first date, kiss, etc.

"Did I really make the right decision here? Could we just have been friends?" he said to himself.

He thought about all of this as he picked up the food for him and mom. In the end, he realized his decision was right. One Scripture seemed to confirm this truth: “Brethren, I count not myself to have apprehended: but this one thing I do, forgetting those things which are behind, and reaching forth unto those things which are before, I press toward the mark for the prize of the high calling of God in Christ Jesus.” [4]

Chapter 8 - Purpose

It was Saturday when George decided to meet DeMarcus again. This time they met in Central Park near Columbus Circle. The cool, brisk fall air was a relief to the summer that NY just went through. The leaves were beginning to change to their familiar yellow and orange and the park had a relaxed Saturday feel to it.

George wanted to walk with his new protege.

“How’s the confession and giving been going?” he asked.

“Good,” DeMarcus started. “No duffle bags of money appeared out of thin air. But it’s been good.”

“Well it usually doesn’t work that way,” George laughed. “But if that does happen...don’t forget about the people who helped you on the come up.”

They both laughed.

“No, but seriously DeMarcus, have you noticed anything since you've started confessing?”

“Well...it’s weird, but I don’t feel as broke. Nothing has changed in my account. I’m starting to have this belief that no matter what happens, God’s got me and I’ll be fine. I guess I am being rescripted.”

“And what about the giving?” George asked.

“Well besides having less money, I haven’t seen anything yet. The one thing I will say and I told my mom yesterday; I think it’s time for me to start looking for new work.”

“Really, why?”

"I don't know. She's been talking about that job not having any opportunities to move up. She's right. I guess I'm just starting to see it. I'm not sure what I'm going to do, but I know my time at the bookstore is coming to an end."

"Hmmm...ok." They walked in silence for a while. "Hey," George said. "Did you eat?"

"Not really."

"Let's stop by this diner off 7th avenue and grab some food."

They made their way to the diner. After they sat down George asked, "How's your friend?"

"Who?" DeMarcus asked, startled.

"Your friend who was having the lust problem. Did you give them the Scriptures I gave you?"

"Oh yeah. Yeah. I did. I know it's helped him a lot with that problem. Thanks for that."

"No problem," George said as he looked at the menu. "You know DeMarcus sometimes struggles are just unmade decisions in disguise."

"Wait, what? What do you mean?" DeMarcus looked away from his own menu to George.

"For the believer at least...struggles or addictions are just unmade decisions. Let me explain..." Before he could, a very nice waitress came over: "Are you two handsome gentlemen ready to order?"

They both made their orders, thanked the waitress, and George continued:

"...so when we get saved by the power of God, we're free from sin. Sin no longer has dominion over our lives. Of course, we're not sinless, but we're not under sin's control like we once were. But we do have certain sins that we 'struggle' with but in Christ, we do have freedom from them. For instance, let's take your friend. He probably struggled with lust because he loved the feel and pleasure it gave. Would you agree?"

"Agreed," DeMarcus said sheepishly.

"And God as good as He is was probably working with him to bring him out of it. But when your friend makes a firm decision to stop, it will stop. He'll guard and fix his thoughts on pure things. He'll cut off communication with the person tempting with lust. And he'll stop going to places that promote lust. Again, it boils down to a decision."

"Hmmm...you make it sound so easy," DeMarcus said with a little doubt.

"I didn't say it was easy, DeMarcus, but it IS simple. One of the root meanings of the word 'decision' is 'to cut off.' When someone REALLY makes a decision regarding something, they are cutting off all other options except that thing." George paused for a minute. "I'll tell you a story..."

DeMarcus smiled. He knew George couldn't control himself.

"...there was a commander of 600 men who landed in enemy territory. The enemy outnumbered his men and had resources his men didn't. When he landed, he decided to burn the ships that carried them. With the ships in flames, he addressed his men: 'You see the boats going up in smoke. That means that we cannot leave these shores alive unless we win! We now have no choice - we win or we perish!' Guess what happened? They won. That's what I mean by making a decision."

"Hmmm...good point," DeMarcus said, nodding his head.

The waitress came back with their food. They took a few moments to eat and drink. After that DeMarcus spoke up: "So when you make a firm decision, you cut all sources of retreat?"

"Yes," George started. If someone decides to be healthy, they'll be healthy. If they decide to be holy, they'll be holy. If they decide to be pure, they'll be pure. And if they decide to live a lust-free life, they'll live a lust-free life."

DeMarcus sat there taking in every word George had said. He was right. He could've stopped his affair with Ebony a LONG TIME ago if he wanted to. But he didn't make the decision to stop. He struggled with it because he loved it and didn't want to give it up.

"DeMarcus," George suddenly spoke up. "Sometime ago you asked me why I created my company and why I stepped down from leading it. When I was younger, I knew I wanted to be involved in ministry. I wasn't a preacher. I couldn't sing. I was so confused. I prayed and prayed and prayed. No answer. One night at NY Pentecostal--when it was still a storefront--there was a guest preacher. He was a missionary raising funds for an orphanage overseas. He was on fire. He talked about everything he was believing God for: the orphanages, a school, staff, evangelizing the area, and et--."

DeMarcus cut him off. "So you're trying to find your way and they're asking you for money," he chuckled.

This time George didn't laugh. He gave DeMarcus a stern look. "Are you going to let me finish?"

"Sorry."

"So anyway he was talking about everything he was believing God for. Then he said, 'Don't think for a minute that I'm someone special God can do great things with one person. If that one person decides to believe God for great things.' And that hit me. It made me realize two things. One, I wanted to do something great for God. And two, I was not called to be a preacher or pastor. But I thought maybe I could help fund the missions of those preachers and pastors."

"Wow. So that's why you started your company?"

"And the main reason I stepped down from running. It was always my goal to build something that could operate apart from me. Once the leadership was strong, I handed over the reins. But what I'm getting at DeMarcus is that this happened when I discovered one thing: my purpose. It was my purpose that drove me to this destination."

DeMarcus sat there taking it all in. He knew George was a committed Christian, but he thought he was all about money. Yes, he was a tither and giver but he did have a strong money consciousness. He couldn't reconcile it. "I honestly thought your overarching goal was to be rich," he said.

"DeMarcus, nothing is wrong with wealth or money. I love the life that I'm able to have for myself and my family. I love the options that money gives me. And I did want to be free financially. But I believe my overarching purpose is to help fund the Gospel. And I think that's why God has blessed me the way He has."

"I'm sure you heard this question before: how do I find my purpose?" DeMarcus asked.

"Well DeMarcus you're wrong: I HAVE NOT heard that question before. The questions I get are: 'how do I become rich?' 'How do I make my first million?' 'What's the secret to your success?' I have NEVER had anyone ask me how do I find purpose. I guess people think that I don't think about things like that. But to answer your question, let's go to the Book." George pulled out his phone and within a minute, found a passage. "Read this."

DeMarcus took the phone, looked at the highlighted passage, and began to read: "'It's in Christ that we find out who we are and what we are living for. Long before we first heard of Christ and got our hopes up, He had His eye on us, had designs on us for glorious living, part of the overall purpose he is working out in everything and everyone.'" [1]

"What do you think it means, DeMarcus?"

"I think it means what it says. We find our purpose in Christ. But it still doesn't answer my question. And I get it: we get our purpose from God. But it's not like I know MY individual purpose."

George thought for a second. And then he looked DeMarcus in the eye "DeMarcus," he started. "Be honest with me, how many times have you asked God what your individual purpose is?"

Now it was DeMarcus' time to think. He knew that he tried to figure out his purpose; he asked others what he thought his purpose was...but he never asked God. Maybe he never thought he'd get an answer. Maybe he thought God didn't want to hear from him because of his relationship with Ebony. Or maybe he thought God wouldn't be interested in helping him figure that out; maybe God wanted him to figure it out on his own. "None. I never asked Him," he finally said.

"Why?"

"I honestly don't know."

"Well, wouldn't the Creator have an idea about the purpose of His creation?"

"Absolutely."

"Look, DeMarcus, when I asked God about my purpose, no answer came from heaven. There was no prophecy spoken over my life. But He guided me to that meeting. So I will say this: once you ask God your purpose, know that it will be found in service and in movement."

"Wait, what?"

"Purpose will be found in service and in movement. Let me explain. Our purpose on this earth is about serving God and serving other people. It's how we find the most joy and fulfillment. In fact, that's all that business is: serving people for a profit. Or fixing problems for a profit. Does that make sense?

"That does. That's actually a pretty good definition of business too. I don't get the movement part though."

"It was tricky for me. Most people say they're going to discover their purpose in a cave, in meditation, or something like that. And they're scared to do the 'wrong' thing. But oftentimes, one thing can lead you to THE thing. David discovered his kingship while tending sheep, Paul discovered his purpose on the way to Damascus road, Peter discovered his purpose while operating his fishing business,

Samuel discovered it while serving Eli. In other words, it's easier to steer a moving car than a parked one. So it was while I was actively seeking my purpose that God led me to the place where I could discover it."

DeMarcus thought about that last thing George said. The truth is he was interested in discovering his purpose, but never actively committed to it. Now he had questions.

"So are you saying that purpose was the reason for your success?"

"No," George started. "There is never just ONE thing that contributes to success. That's like saying the reason for Michael Jordan's success was that he was competitive. Well, he could be competitive and not be fast, or strong, or have a good ball handle, have stamina, endurance, a good three-point shot, and etc. Remember: success leaves clues, not A clue. There are many things that contribute to success. Purpose was one of the things that contributed to mine. Now I will say this: it is possible to become wealthy and 'successful' and not understand purpose. The problem is when you go after money and 'success' there is the illusion that they give meaning. It's not true. People get money, realize that it doesn't bring meaning, and then look for another 'high.' And in due time, it all comes crashing down."

"'Vanity of vanity,' says the Preacher, vanity of vanities! All is vanity,'" [2] DeMarcus said.

"That's right."

"So then what are the benefits of purpose?"

"Hmmmm." George thought about the question. He reached for his phone, found his Bible app, and was looking for a Scripture. He found it. "DeMarcus read this for me, the highlighted parts." DeMarcus took the phone. He was getting more and more used to these informal Bible studies. Even though George had no desire to be a preacher or pastor...he would've made a good Bible teacher.

DeMarcus started: "We, however, will not boast beyond measure, but within the limits of the sphere which God appointed us—a sphere which especially includes you. For we are not overextending ourselves (as though our authority did not extend to you), for it was to you that we came with the gospel of Christ; not boasting of things beyond measure, that is, in other men's labors, but having hope, that as your faith is increased, we shall be greatly enlarged by you in our sphere, to preach the gospel in the regions beyond you, and not to boast in another man's sphere of accomplishment." [3]

"Now here's what I want to point out," George started as he took his phone back from DeMarcus. The first thing is the word 'sphere.' How many times do you read it in that passage?"

DeMarcus took a minute to count. "Four."

"That's right. Now that word 'sphere' in Greek comes from the word 'kanon' which means 'a boundary or place of activity.' When you understand your purpose, you understand your boundaries and your place of activity. You know who you are and who you are not. Your greatest fulfillment, achievement, and success will be found in your 'sphere.' Not someone else's. It's when we get outside of our purpose that we waste time and energy being someone we weren't meant to be—building someone else's dream and their vision. Another benefit of purpose is it gives needed direction.

George started looking through his phone again for a Scripture. He found and handed the phone to DeMarcus. "Read the highlighted one."

DeMarcus grabbed the phone and read: "The noble hearted man has noble purposes and by these he will be guided." [4]

"Purpose is always going to steer you in the way of destiny," George said. "Most people try to get a vision for their lives without seeking purpose first. And you can achieve a lot but not achieve something meaningful. It's like the story of a group of men cutting their way through the jungle with machetes. They're cutting through the undergrowth, clearing it out. Then one of the men climbs the tallest tree, surveys the entire situation, and yells, 'Wrong jungle!' How do the other men respond? 'Shut up! We're making progress.'"

They both laugh.

"I hope you get what I'm saying, DeMarcus..."

"...yeah," DeMarcus interjected. "You can make a lot of progress and be in the wrong jungle. Or you can achieve a lot and not be in your purpose."

"Exactly. And you can get outside of your 'sphere' and it leads to problems."

"What do you mean?"

George thought for a moment. "Have you ever heard of Hobby Lobby?"

"No."

"Well it's a retail chain headquartered in Oklahoma City. Their founder is David Green. He's a Christian man known for his generosity and stewardship. He built his business by glorifying God and sticking to his 'sphere.' But in the 1980's he got off track. During the 80's there was a prolonged oil boom with a lot of free-flowing cash. With all that cash, people could have sold anything and made a profit. So what did Green do? He started selling expensive luggage, grandfather clocks, ceiling fans, gourmet foods, and even miniature brass oil rigs."

"Sounds like he made a good profit. What's the problem?"

"The problem was that he strayed out of his 'sphere.' He just didn't know it yet because the cash was covering his mistake. Then there was an oil bust in 1985, the money dried up, and by the end of the year, he lost nearly a million dollars."

"Whoa."

"Yup. The bank threatened to call their note, suppliers started cutting them off, and he didn't know what to do. So he reached out to God and in time, God gave him direction. According to Green,

God told him he needed to get back to his core business, or his 'sphere.' And he did. He also cut expenses, found a different lender, and worked out deals with their suppliers. By the end of 1986, they were out of the red and were earning a profit again." [5]

"I mean that sounds great and all," DeMarcus started. "But if I'm being a devil's advocate, was that really just fixed with prayer? I'm sure any business consultant or other business person would see that: go back to what worked, cut your expenses, and find another lender. I'm not saying God didn't tell him what to do...I am saying the answer sounds obvious."

"Hmmmm...I see where you're coming from...and you're right when you look at it it does sound obvious. And God does often give 'obvious' answers. But what about the answers that are not so obvious?"

"What do you mean?"

"Well...the Scriptures say that God's Ways are not our ways and His Thoughts are not our thoughts. [6] So oftentimes, His answer is above our reasoning. It's not always something you can figure out. For instance, have you ever heard of Gary and Drenda Keesee?"

"No. Who are they?" By this time DeMarcus had finished his food and was looking at the dessert menu. George jumped in, "Where are you putting all this stuff??"

"Hey," DeMarcus said, patting his stomach. "I didn't have any breakfast and you wanted to meet early soooo..." He looked at George and shrugged.

"Anyway. Gary and Drenda Keesee are pastors and business owners. Before they became business owners, they were in a financial mess: they had finance company loans, owed thousands in back taxes, owed thousands to relatives, owed money on two rusted cars, had judgments against them, and liens. Basically, they owed everyone money. Then, one day an attorney called demanding payment. They had no more credit or credibility--they were stuck."

"So what did he do?" DeMarcus asked.

"I don't know. What would you do? What's the 'obvious' answer here?"

DeMarcus thought for a while. Clearly, George was trying to teach him a lesson...and was succeeding. If he had no money, no credit, and couldn't borrow from anyone, how could he pay that money? He had no answer.

"Ok...ok...I get it. Some problems have no 'obvious' answers. You win. What did they do?"

"Glad you asked," George began. "Gary reached out to God, God showed him the error of his ways, he repented, and together he and his wife determined to use no more debt. The next day a car that he owed money on burned up. He paid off the car, the attorney, and some needed bills with the insurance money. Not your 'obvious' answer. Here's also a not so 'obvious' answer: God told Gary to start a business helping people get out of debt."

"Wait what now?" DeMarcus said, startled. "I thought you said Gary and his wife were in suffocating debt. So how could they start a business helping people get out of debt?"

"I know it makes no sense. But like the Bible says, God uses foolish things to confound the wise.[7] He created a company helping people get out of debt and that company helped him and his family get out of debt. DeMarcus, all I'm saying is this: God knows your purpose and it's up to you to discover what that purpose is."

DeMarcus just sat there and thought about everything George said. Every time he spoke to or listened to George, he realized how little he knew. It was as if every conversation was changing him, molding him into a different man. This man was by every standard 'successful,' yet he loved God and was committed to His Will. He had never seen this before. He wanted what George had and was now committed to becoming that kind of man.

"One thing I want you to remember, DeMarcus," George said, breaking his thoughts. "True purpose is found in service. We are here to serve, not be served. So when you do discover God's purpose for your life, it will ALWAYS be rooted in that."

"Purpose is found in service, got it," DeMarcus said.

George looked at DeMarcus and smiled. Mission accomplished. He raised his hand and asked for the check.

Chapter 9 - Vision

George and DeMarcus left the diner and continued their walk in Central Park. The day was warmer and the park was filled with more tourists and residents. The busyness gave the park the splendor it was known for. DeMarcus walked in silence as he tried to digest everything George said over breakfast. It was so counter-cultural. DeMarcus had read some self-help books and the one thing that seemed to stand out with all of them was: vision.

"Have a strong vision."

"If you can see it, you can achieve it."

"If you create a vision for your life, doors will open."

"Whatever the mind of man can conceive and believe, the mind can achieve."

And yet George's approach was different: renew your mind with God's Word, give and give cheerfully, and now purpose. The question DeMarcus had was: where does vision come into this? Was it necessary? Was it needed?

"George," he started. "You talked a lot about purpose; what about vision?"

"What do you mean?"

"Well, vision is always the thing talked about with successful people. 'He had a vision.' Or, 'she had a vision.' But you're talking about things like 'purpose.' Does having a vision even matter?"

"Good question," George started. "Let's take a seat." They walked over to a nearby bench and sat down. "So...I think you forgot what I said in the diner. There are many things that contribute to success, but there is a difference between 'success' and 'good success.' Unfortunately, there are going to be many 'successful' people living an eternal existence apart from God. To gain the whole world and lose your soul is not 'successful living.' But here's what I did not explain..."

George took out a business card and a pen and started to draw. When he finished, he showed it to DeMarcus:

PURPOSE----->VISION----->PURPOSE.

DeMarcus looked at it, looked at George, then looked back at it. "Okaaaay?"

George chuckled. "DeMarcus, good success always starts with purpose: knowing WHO you are and WHOSE you are. But out of that purpose flows vision. And the purpose of the vision is to fulfill the original purpose. Let me explain: I knew one of my purposes was to help fund the Gospel. From that purpose came the vision for my company. But the purpose of my vision (my company) was to fulfill my original purpose (fund the gospel). Does that make sense?"

"It does. I get it."

"So vision is important," George continued. "But also understand that vision is both inside out and outside in."

"Wait what?" DeMarcus asked, startled. "What do you mean it's 'inside out' and 'outside in'? I don't get that."

"I was confused too when I heard that. This time I'm going to read something for you. It's from the 'Sermon on the Mount,' but it's in the Message Translation." George said as he reached for his phone. He scrolled for a little bit. "Where is it? Where is it? Ah...there it is. 'You're blessed when you get your inside world—your mind and heart—put right. Then you can see God in the outside world.'[1]

What we see outside is often a reflection of who we are inside DeMarcus. For example, the positive see a positive world, the negative see a negative world, cheaters see a world of cheaters, and so on. People who cheat in relationships tend to be the ones accusing the other of cheating. Why? They're projecting their own infidelity. You see what you are."

"Whoa! Okaaayyy...Dr.Phil-Oprah-with-a-side-of-TD Jakes- undercover billionaire...that was heavy!"

They both let out a laugh.

"That's why," George started again. "You should never take too seriously the comments of others: 'you're too fat,' 'you're too stupid,' 'you're too skinny,' 'you're too ugly,' and etc. Often these aren't accurate reflections but inaccurate projections. Comments like these usually come from the insecurities of the people making them. The insecure will always tear down while the secure will always build up.

And that's why many parents who never received love and affirmation in their youth tend to be overly critical of their own children. They find it hard to show love or any kind of support. Why? You can only give what you have. So when God gets ready to change us, the first thing He does is change us from the inside: He helps us to see who we are in Him. Only from there do we have any chance of 'good success.'"

"I honestly don't see how that translates to 'good success' or any success. If I'm being honest," DeMarcus said.

George thought for a minute. "Let's say a person was trying to lose weight. They find a successful program and eating regimen. And let's say that they lost weight...a good amount of weight. Success right? Not necessarily. If their habits don't change, their environment doesn't change, and how they view themselves don't change, they'll go back to who they were. If they ONLY see themselves as a 'fat' person they'll find a way to become who they see. But what if they--in addition to working on their body--decided to change how they see themselves? What if they truly saw themselves as a lean, fit person? They'd do the things that lean fit people do?"

"Hmmm...I see that. That makes sense. But does that really apply to 'good success?'"

George smiled. Pulled out his phone and started scrolling. He handed the phone to DeMarcus: "Read this."

"It's almost like you were waiting for that question, huh?" DeMarcus said. "Let's see... 'The land through which we have gone as spies is a land that devours its inhabitants, and all the people whom we saw in it are men of great stature. There we saw the giants, and we were like grasshoppers in our own sight, and so we were in their sight.'" [2]

DeMarcus handed the phone back to George.

"Two people can be looking at the exact same thing but see something totally different," George started. "When Moses sent out twelve spies to view the Promised Land, they saw the same thing but had a mixed interpretation. Caleb and Joshua believed they could have it but the other men thought they couldn't. The majority gave a horrible report based not on how they viewed the situation..."

"...but on how they viewed themselves," DeMarcus interjected.

"Exactly!" George said. "You can't have real 'good success' with low self-worth. Remember what Paul said, 'I can do all things through Christ who strengthens me.' [3] There has to be a belief in God and a belief in yourself. You have to believe you can do it with His help. And that's why God works with us on our inside-out vision. And He also helps us with our outside-in vision."

They both took a minute to view the busyness of the city. Children were running around; parents were shouting and telling them not to run too far, the ice cream truck had a swarm of children around it, tourists were taking pictures of the city and its wonders, and on and on. It was ceaseless activity - unmeasured and unmeasurable.

"George, why are you telling me all this? Why are you teaching ME?"

"Why do you ask? Don't you deserve to be taught?"

"No I mean why ME? You have a company, a family, and I'm sure many other things you could be doing this Saturday. So why are you spending it teaching me?"

George thought for a moment.

"DeMarcus, I grew up in Queens to a single mom. My dad left us when I was 13 years old. After he left, it almost seemed like her mind left with him. It wasn't that she didn't feed, clothe, or shelter us (I have two other siblings) it was that her behavior became more erratic. I think one of the things that is often unsaid in the black community is the toxic mother. The truth is, she had more stress than she knew how to handle and took it out on us. I didn't know how to respond when that happened: I felt abandoned by my dad and suffocated by my mom. She meant well but she didn't have the emotional bandwidth to raise children on her own. I got in trouble I didn't need to get into, hung around people I shouldn't have, and was just a hurt black boy. God saved me at nineteen, but I still struggled with knowing who I was. I struggled with manhood. You don't have that DeMarcus. You have a mom who loves and has the bandwidth to raise you right. And she has the wisdom to know her limitations: she can't raise a man."

"So you tryna to raise me?" DeMarcus was shocked at the tone that came out. He didn't mean to say it like that. He wasn't trying to be raised. There was only one man who could do that and he wasn't here.

George stiffened slightly. "No. I'm not trying to 'raise' you. I have my own children to raise. I'm trying to 'help' you. Let's get that straight."

"Hey look...I didn't mean it like that," DeMarcus started apologetically. "I do appreciate everything you're doing. You're right; my mom is dope and so was my dad. He didn't leave us...he was taken."

"What do you mean 'taken?'"

"He was taken. God took him. I don't know why but it is what it is. You're not supposed to question the Big Man, right?"

"Hmmm...you think God killed your Dad?" George sat there for a minute, thinking about the enormity of that statement and the hurt behind it. "DeMarcus, how do you trust a God that 'killed' your dad?" George asked softly.

DeMarcus shifted in his seat. George touched a nerve. "Good question." They both sat in silence for a while.

George looked at the ice cream truck. "I know you're probably still hungry," he said with a slight chuckle. "Let's grab some ice cream." DeMarcus nodded as they walked over to the ice cream truck. Even as they waited in line to order, the question still rang in his mind: How do you trust a God who took away your dad? He could only come up with one real honest answer: you don't.

After DeMarcus and George got their ice cream, they walked back to the bench and sat down. They ate for a little bit admiring the scenery, then DeMarcus broke the silence: "So why me?"

"Your mother asked. You listen, ask good questions, and implement. If you didn't listen, wanted to do your own thing, or 'knew more' than me I would not waste my time," George said plainly. "Fair?"

"Yeah. Appreciate that," DeMarcus said. "So back to vision...vision is inside out, I get that. What do you mean by 'outside in?'"

George thought for a moment. "For this one, I'll use the example of Moses. Moses spent a lot of time in the Presence of God. It was there he vented his frustrations, acknowledged his weaknesses, and received orders on what to do next. When he came from His Presence, he was unaware that his face was radiant. So because of his face, he covered it with a veil in the presence of the people but uncovered it in the Presence of God. Moses saw the radiance of God and became radiant himself. The point is this: when you focus on something for a long period of time, you not only attract it but you reflect it. When you focus on better, you become better; when you focus on greater, you become greater; when you focus on wealth you become wealthier, and so on."

George grabbed his phone, scrolled through his Bible app, and handed the phone to DeMarcus. "Read that." DeMarcus put the ice cream cup on the bench, took the phone, and started to read:

"But friends, that's exactly who we are: children of God. And that's only the beginning. Who knows how we'll end up! What we know is that when Christ is openly revealed, we'll see Him—and in seeing Him, become like Him." [4]

He handed the phone back to George. "That's a good one. We become what we focus on."

"Exactly," George said. "From a spiritual standpoint, this is how God works: He first changes us from the inside out—changing our spirits, hearts, and minds so that we can see Him better. And then changes us from the outside in—tells us to focus on Him, His Word, and His promises so that we can become more like Him. From a practical standpoint as it relates to outside-in vision, I focused all my attention on what I wanted...not on what I didn't want. I wanted a company that would change the world and allow me to fund ministries, I wanted a family that I could love and take care of, and I wanted to be the man I didn't have growing up."

"What do you mean not focusing on the things you DIDN'T want?" DeMarcus asked.

"I mean exactly that. I didn't focus on lack, failure, family dysfunction, and etc. Don't get me wrong, there was plenty of failure and lack along the way and I still have some family dysfunction. But I refused to let that be my focus. Let me say it this way: there's a reason why a company with a deeply entrenched long-term vision blows past competitors whose only ambition is to remain open. There's a reason why resources, influence, and opportunity seem to tackle the man or woman of committed vision, why simultaneously dodging those who aren't sure of what they want."

"Hmmmmm...." DeMarcus thought to himself about George's statement. He had a vague fuzzy idea of what he wanted for his life but it wasn't a committed vision. Ever since his dad died, he was just floating through life--unsure of what he wanted and who he was. He couldn't do that anymore. He couldn't BE this kind of man anymore. It was time HE became that person of purpose and vision. "So how is outside vision practical?"

"We'll get to that," George said. "Let's go for a walk."

They began their journey again in the city. The conversation was light: sports (both men were basketball fans), the weather, finding out about each other's respective families, and so on. DeMarcus discovered that George was married for over 20 years with 3 kids. From what he could tell, the marriage was good as George spoke very highly about his wife. They found their way to a local coffee shop. Even though it was almost 11 o'clock, it wasn't crowded. They sat down.

"DeMarcus, real vision is always realized with goals," George said. "And the problem with most people is that they have dreams...vision...but no goals."

"You sound like a motivational speaker," DeMarcus said with a chuckle.

"Well yeah, I guess I do," George responded with a laugh. "But seriously having no goals is not a laughing matter. There's a reason the Bible talks about writing the vision and making it plain.[5] There's also a reason why it's said the people with no goals work for the people that do. But real goal setting is always focused. I'm gonna get some coffee. Do you want anything?"

"No. I'm good. Thank you."

He looked around the coffee shop taking in the music, the people, and the decor. Today has truly been an interesting day. He learned so much from George...he just needed to figure out how to put it into practice. Purpose. Vision. Inside out. Outside In. Goals.

George returned to the table with his coffee, a piece of paper, and a pen.

"Purpose is something that will be revealed over time," he started. "God will show it to you through prayer, Scripture, or some problem that needs to be solved in the world." George said as he slid the paper and pen to DeMarcus. "But goals can be worked on now. I want you to write 10 things you want to accomplish in the next 5 years. It can be anything you want. But understand that if you accomplished these 10 things, it would drastically change your life.

But don't worry how you can afford it, don't look at what you've accomplished so far...stretch yourself, AND let it be things that scare you a bit."

George got ready to walk away; he turned around and said, "Remember 10 things that if you accomplished them would change your life. I'm gonna go for a walk...I'll be back in..." he looked at his watch. "25 minutes. Have those 10 things written down."

He walked off.

DeMarcus looked at George as he left. He then stared at the sheet of paper. What would he write? What did he want? This makes no sense. He picked up the pen. Slowly ideas of what he really wanted started to formulate in his mind. Some were things he could do if he worked really hard. If he really pushed himself. Some were things he wanted but could see no way of accomplishing. He started to write.

After taking in the scenery of the park, having his own devotion and making one or two needed business calls, George walked back into the coffee shop. He found DeMarcus on his phone and the piece of paper in front of him. He sat down. DeMarcus put his phone down. George picked up the piece of paper and read.

"Ok. These are good. Here's what you do next. Circle the one that matters the most to you. The one that if you accomplished would TRULY change your life," he said.

George slid the piece of paper back to DeMarcus. He looked at George with a "are-you-serious-right-now" kind of look. It took him nearly half an hour to come up with these and now he wanted the most "important" one. DeMarcus looked at his list. He looked at each one carefully and the answer jumped out at him. He circled it and handed the paper to George.

"It wouldn't just change MY life," he said.

George looked at the paper and smiled. "'Buy my momma a house.' Why that one?"

"Well, a few reasons. You're right she is a good mom--she deserves it. Second, I know she's been wanting to move out of that apartment for a while. And the main reason is...I've heard her praying to God about it for a while. She ends up thanking Him in advance, but I know she wishes she had it. I want it for her. She deserves it."

"Good. Is the house going to be in NY?" George took the pen and paper and started writing as he asked this.

"Yeah. Long Island. I know she doesn't want to leave NY. But I know she wants to be in a more suburban area."

"And how many bedrooms is this house going to have?"

"I think 3 should be adequate. Maybe a 3 bedroom 2 bathroom house."

"And you're looking to have this house in 5 years?"

"Yeah. I don't know how. But that's the time frame you said, right?"

"I did. But do YOU think it's doable?"

DeMarcus took a minute to think that over. "Well...a lot can happen in 5 years."

"Good answer. Just to recap: in 5 years, you're looking to buy a 3 bedroom 2 bathroom house in Long Island for your mom. Congratulations! You have set a worthy goal."

"Why the congratulations? I haven't achieved anything yet." DeMarcus asked, confused.

"No...you actually have. More than 90 percent of people don't have goals. They have wishes and desires. The fact that you have something specific and time-based is half the battle. Now, this is where outside-in vision comes in.

"What do you mean?" DeMarcus asked.

"Well, I'll use me as an example," George started. "My first major goal was to make one million dollars in a calendar year. I wanted to make sure I had my mind on that goal all the time. So I bought a million-dollar bill and kept it in my bedroom. I wrote that goal and kept it by my bed. I broke down what a million-dollar year looked like by month, week, and day and put it in a place I could always see it. I wanted my eye on the prize. It didn't matter what was going on, I was always focused on the goal. In fact..." George pulled out his phone, found a Scripture, and handed it to DeMarcus. "Read this."

“I was wondering when that Bible was going to come out again,” DeMarcus said as he took the phone. He looked at the highlighted verses and read out loud. “‘Keep your eyes straight ahead; ignore all sideshow distractions. Watch your step, and the road will stretch out smooth before you. Look neither right nor left; leave evil in the dust.’[6] How do you find all this???” DeMarcus said, handing George his phone.

“Gotta study to show yourself approved. But either way, if I were you and I had that goal, I’d do everything to keep that goal in front of me. I would keep a picture of the house on my phone and computer. I’d drive in the neighborhoods. I’d find out about the taxes, the upkeep, and current prices. I would learn how the home buying process works and what programs could help me as a first- time homebuyer. But... the Bible says to build your business before you build your house. In other words, you need to prioritize the sources of income before the comforts of income.

“Wait, what? Where does the Bible say that?”

“It’s another version of Proverbs 24. Here, read it yourself.” George said, handing DeMarcus his phone. “‘Develop your business first before building your house.’[7] Wow! Crazy.”

He said as he handed back the phone.

“Yup. That Scripture has aided with many decisions: personal and corporate. But if the goal is to get a house for your mom in 5 years, that’s where I’d start. But I do have a serious question for you: are you interested in achieving this goal or are you committed to it?”

“What do you mean ‘interested’ or ‘committed’? What’s the difference?”

"There's actually a very big difference. To be interested in a goal is to do what you have to do when it's convenient. To be committed to a goal is to do what you have to do when it's NOT convenient. And let me tell you: I didn't build the company, life, or family I have by being 'interested' in my goals. I was committed. So again I ask you: are you 'interested' or 'committed?'"

DeMarcus sat there for a while. He really contemplated the question. How could he buy his mother a house? How could he afford it? He had no job prospects. He didn't have a successful company like George. Not to mention he'd never done anything like this before. But then he thought about his mom; everything she had given up for him; how great a relationship they had; how much she wanted to leave that Brooklyn apartment. He had to do something. 5 years was going to come anyway whether he had the house or not."

"Committed," he said.

"Good! I have a homework assignment for you. We're going to meet next week. Same diner. But this time for lunch." George took the sheet of paper and started to write as he spoke. "You have some homework: First, I want you to find every Scripture you can on owning a home. I don't care about the version. We are going to pray about it next week. The Promises of God are yes and amen [8] so we're going to go to God based on His Promises.

Second, I want you to find out which part of Long Island you want to live in: Nassau or Suffolk. That one you'll have to find out from Mom without her knowing what you're doing.

Third, find out current home prices.

Fourth, get an idea of how you're going to pay for this. Will it be as an employee or business owner?"

George looked at his watch. “I do have to go. I have a meeting at the Time Warner building near Columbus Circle. I’ll see you next week.”

And like that he was gone.

DeMarcus was lost in thought: Can I do this? How am I going to do this? Is this even possible? Are there Scriptures that even relate to this? Isn’t this God’s responsibility? Why can’t her Dad do this?

Another thought was forming in his head. George had done so much in their time spent together; he opened his eyes to so much. But George couldn’t do what he did for everyone. DeMarcus got the impression he didn’t want to. He was just the exception to the rule. What if he could share the truths George was teaching him. He didn’t know the majority of this stuff--chances are there are other men that didn’t know either.

Chapter 10 - Underwriting

The week was like a blur for DeMarcus.

It was the busiest he had been in a LONG time. He scoured the Bible and the internet for Scriptures related to homeownership. He was shocked to find so many. It seemed the more he really looked into the Bible the more he could see its practicality. Before he only saw it as a religious book used on Sunday that was a mandatory read. But he was starting to realize it dealt with so many things: purpose, finance, family, direction, and so on.

It really was the Book of Life.

He also had to play detective asking his mom the kind of house she wanted. He would ask a few questions a day so as to not tip her off. But soon enough she got tired of the investigation: "Boy, why do you want to know about my house? Are you playing the lottery?!"

Even with her being annoyed, he got the info he needed: she wanted to live in Nassau, wanted a 3 bedroom 2 bathroom house (the extra room for guests), a garden, and a basement. He started looking at some programs and realized George was right: there were a lot of good ones for first-time homebuyers. He jotted them down and decided he would do more in-depth research the following week. As well as checking out possible neighborhoods.

Now as to the question of a business owner or employee: he loved the lifestyle that George was able to afford but wasn't quite ready for that level of responsibility. Being an employee seemed a more viable option considering the time frame. He also knew for certain that he needed a career change.

The other idea of teaching other young men what George showed him didn't leave either. He didn't know how he was going to do it, but he felt strongly about it. The answer would come when it came; he just had to be ready for it.

He thought about all of this as he sat in the diner waiting for George. It was 11:55 am. He didn't want to be late for this next meeting. He sat in a booth nursing a cup of coffee. He hadn't spoken to George since last Saturday. There was no need to. The only thing that needed to be done was the assignment. He did that. Now the next step was the next step.

He sat for a few more minutes quietly looking at his phone and George walked in at 12:01 pm.

"You're late," DeMarcus said with mocked seriousness.

"I'm sorry 'boss' it won't happen again. Glad to see you're here on time."

"Well, I didn't think it'd be a good look to show up late."

"Good call. How was your week?"

"Busy. In a good way."

"Well, those are the best kinds of busy. That means you were productive. What did you accomplish?"

"Well I did most of my 'homework,'" DeMarcus started. "The only thing I wasn't able to do was drive through the neighborhoods. There are so many neighborhoods in Nassau. I'll have to tackle that this upcoming week. You know this feels really good. I mean...it feels good to be...going somewhere. Do you know what I mean?"

George gave him a look that said, Yeah silly...I know what you mean. "Well, you should feel good," he said. "The brain is actually a goal seeking mechanism. It gets the greatest pleasure from meeting objectives. That's why the process of goal setting is so powerful...many believers don't realize that. They're just waiting for God to do everything. It doesn't work like that. Of course, we're going to pray and believe, but then we're going to get to work. And if you stay committed to this goal you'll see resources that were always there."

"What do you mean?" DeMarcus asked.

"Well from a spiritual standpoint, God will help you. He's always a present Help. [1]

From a natural standpoint, the brain receives millions of bits of information per second and that information goes through a filtering process—keeping some and deleting others. The brain has a filter. It's called the Reticular Activation System - it decides what to accept and what to reject based on values, beliefs, and prejudices. The brain will only accept information that reinforces deeply held beliefs and reject those that don't. So now that you have this vision and this vision is made plain with goals, the RAS is activated to notice resources and filter in anything that will help achieve that goal. Again: the resources were always there but never noticed. There's a proverb that says, 'A man can walk in a forest and still not find timber wood'"

"Or when the student is ready the teacher will appear," DeMarcus interjected.

George looked at DeMarcus, the way a teacher would a most improved student. "Exactly. Anyway, let's see your Scriptures." DeMarcus took out a folded sheet of paper and handed it to George. George took a minute to read it over. "I'm impressed. You did your research."

Scriptures for New Home

Isaiah 65:21: They shall build homes and inhabit them; and they shall plant vineyards, and eat the fruit of them.

Proverbs 12:7 (AMPC): The wicked are overthrown and are not, but the house of the [uncompromisingly] righteous shall stand.

Proverbs 24:27 (AMP): [Put first things first.] Prepare your work outside and get it ready for yourself in the field; and afterward build your house and establish a home.

Jeremiah 29:5 (AMP): "Build yourselves houses and dwell in them; plant gardens and eat the fruit of them.

Psalms 107:7 (AMP): He led them forth by the straight and right way, that they might go to a city where they could establish their homes.

Psalms 107:7 (MSG): He put your feet on a wonderful road that took you straight to a good place to live.

Psalms 18:19 (NIV): He brought me out into a spacious place: He rescued me because He delighted in me.

Psalms 66:12 (NIV): You let people ride over our heads; we went through fire and water, but You brought us to a place of abundance.

2 Samuel 7:10(NIV) And I will provide a place for my people Israel and will plant them so that they can have a home of their own and no longer be disturbed. Wicked people will not oppress them anymore, as they did at the beginning

2 Samuel 7:11 (NIV) ...The Lord declares to you that the Lord himself will establish a house for you.

Isaiah 32:18 (MSG): My people will live in a peaceful neighborhood – in safe houses, in quiet gardens.

"Thanks," DeMarcus said. "It's kind of like what you said: when I found one, others began to appear."

"Good stuff. We'll pray later. But...let me look at this menu...I am starving."

While looking at the menu, the waitress came. Both George and DeMarcus knew what they wanted. She pleasantly took their orders and left.

"Oh," George started. "Did you find out how you were going to pay for this?"

"Yes. As much as I love what you've accomplished, I think it will be as an employee. Right now I don't have the bandwidth to build a company as you did. I think a career change is needed though."

"Good. And that is fine. Remember this always: we're paid for how much value we bring to the marketplace; and how many problems we solve. I'm paid what I'm paid because of all the value my company brings and the problems we solve. You can add immense value as an employee or entrepreneur. And be paid handsomely either way. That choice is yours. But...now that you have your vision and goals, you need to move to the next step."

"Which is?" DeMarcus asked.

"Finding a mentor."

"Why is that important?"

"When you know what you want or what you're going after, the next step is to find someone who's done it," George said. "Remember, I told you earlier: success leaves clues. You want to get to success as fast as humanly possible. You don't do that by reinventing the wheel. No. You find a person who's done it and then copy them. It's exactly what God did through Jesus."

"What do you mean?"

George took out his phone and began scrolling. After a few seconds, he handed the phone to DeMarcus. "Read this." DeMarcus put down the water he was sipping and took the phone. He read, "'For even hereunto were ye called: because Christ also suffered for us, leaving us an example, that ye should follow His steps.' [2] Ok?"

"Do you know what that word 'example' means?" George asked as he took back his phone. Without waiting for an answer, he responded. "It is the Greek word 'Hupogrammos.' Yes...HOOP-O-GRAM-OS. It means an underwriting; or copy for imitation.' It comes from the custom of tracing letters for scholars to copy. So when God got ready to show mankind how He wanted them to live, He said, 'Study My Son. Do what He does. He's your copy for imitation. When I learned that, I realized I didn't have to figure it all out, I just needed to follow someone who did what I wanted to do."

DeMarcus took a minute to let that all soak in. Was it really that simple? Pray about what you want, make a goal towards getting it, and find someone who's already done it. Could it really be that simple?

George continued, "It doesn't always have to be ONE mentor. When I was building my business, I didn't just have one mentor. Some mentors I never even met but they were my mentors. What I mean is, I copied certain aspects of their life. For instance: John D. Rockefeller was one of my mentors. I loved his generosity and determination. He was like a pit bull--never quit mentality. I wanted and needed that."

"Soooo...wouldn't you be technically a mentor to me?"

"Yes," George said. "But for your overall growth and development, you need more than one. No one person has all the answers...even me."

"But why would you direct me elsewhere? Why wouldn't you just show me how to get the house?" DeMarcus asked incredulously.

"Two reasons: I didn't buy my first home as an employee but as a business owner. It took a while for me to buy my first home. It wasn't until the business had some legs. Thank God for a patient wife. Second reason: I don't ever want you to rely on one mentor. There's a reason the Bible says in the multitude of counsel there is safety. [3]

At this point, their waitress came over with their orders. She sorted through everything, asked if they needed anything, gave them a pleasant smile, and left.

"But one thing I forgot with goals," George started. "There is one thing I want you to do. First, put your goal in a place where you can see them every day. The one place I recommend is your phone-- primarily your screen saver."

"Why?"

"Well, the average person checks their phone over 250 times a day. So every time you look at your phone, I want you to be reminded of what you're going after. That will give you the focus to work on that major goal every day--in some capacity. The fact that you have a major goal and are working on it every day will put you light years ahead of most people."

"Hmmm. I could see that. I'll do that today."

"Good."

They sat and ate their meal. The lesson was done for the day. They spoke about sports, their respective families, and some questions DeMarcus had about homeownership. After the meal, they went to Central Park where they prayed asking God for the wisdom and finances to get the home.

They spoke a little more, and after that George left. He didn't say when he would see DeMarcus again.

Chapter 11 - The Extra Mile

Another day at the bookstore and DeMarcus was doing his normal work. Since he last saw George, nothing had really changed. There was no grand vision from God on how to get the home. No one stopped by with a bag of money. Everything was still the same.

Did the prayer even work?

George insisted that it had. He said the day they prayed and believed in faith it was already done. But, even though it was already done, the manifestation of it was another story. That would take time, he said. So DeMarcus did what he could do: he did a quick drive into Nassau to get a feel of neighborhoods, he put a picture of a home on his computer and phone screen saver as a reminder, and he started to update his resume.

Still, he felt no closer than when he started.

He thought of all this while he was at the bookstore. He was thinking about this until he saw George walk in. “Ummmm...what are you doing here?” he asked.

“Nice to see you too. I actually wanted to take you to lunch later. Hope I’m not stepping on any plans.”

“I mean...yeah that’s cool.” DeMarcus thought for a second. “Am I in trouble or something?”

“Are you in trouble because I’m taking you to lunch? Yeah, DeMarcus I came to give you your walking papers.” George said with slight sarcasm.

“Ok. Stupid question. I can get off at 11.”

“11 it is. I’ll meet you back here.” And just like that, he did his signature walk-off.

DeMarcus wondered what the surprise meeting meant. I mean George had a busy life. The fact that he took time away from that busy life to come see him had to be for something—no sense in trying to figure it out now.

The time passed by quickly. George came back as he promised. They left and found a Wendy’s nearby. Because it was still before lunch, the restaurant wasn’t as crowded. They ordered their food. When George got ready to pay, DeMarcus put out his hand, “I got this one.”

George stepped back and said nothing. His student was coming into his own. They got their food and sat at a table in a corner--away from the busyness.

“So what did I do?” DeMarcus asked.

“How’s mom? How’s the home search? And did you put the goal in front of you?” George asked, deflecting the question.

“She's good. It’s coming along. And yes. Now...what did I do?”

George chuckled.

“You actually did nothing wrong,” he started. “After we prayed, I thought about what you said regarding the home. I mean, getting the home as an ‘employee.’ I also thought about what you said about making a career change. And I realized that there was an important piece of the puzzle that’s missing. I could’ve called, but I felt it’d be better to do it in person.”

“What’s the missing ‘piece?’” DeMarcus asked as he ate his fries.

George took out his phone, did his familiar scroll and handed the phone to DeMarcus. “Read this.” DeMarcus put down his fries, wiped his hands, and took the phone from George. He read, “And whoever compels you to go one mile, go with him two.”[1] He handed the phone back to George. “Ok?”

“You ever heard of ‘going the extra mile?’” George asked.

“Yeah. Who hasn’t?”

“Well, what you probably don’t know is the term originated here.” He said while pointing at his phone. “It originated with Jesus.”

“Okay?” DeMarcus said, still not getting where George was going.

“When Jesus said it, he related it to an oppressive custom in His day. It originated with the Persian government. Under this custom, the king’s messenger had the power to take horses, camels, and men into service against their will. In fact, messengers were staged in specific locations by the king; if someone passed the post, they would rush out and ‘compel’ them into service.”

“Well, that sucks. So it’s like ‘eminent domain’ except the government isn’t paying for it?”

“Yeah,” George nodded. “And the government is not asking you to carry its stuff as well. But...that very custom was then adopted by the Roman government. Simon of Cyrene was ‘compelled’ to help Jesus with his cross.” [2]

“Oh wow!”

"Yup. So what Jesus advised was countercultural. He said instead of complaining and quarreling about the oppressive practice, exceed expectations in a spirit of love and service.

"So, that's good and all, but I'm still not getting you," DeMarcus said.

"What I'm saying is that going the extra mile is our duty as believers in the workplace. But it is also a POWERFUL promotional tool. Why? Most people only go the first mile; in fact, some don't even go the first mile. The person who can go that extra mile and do more than they are paid becomes indispensable."

"But I'm already a good employee."

"Well… 'good' is not good enough. Not for where you're trying to go and what you're trying to accomplish. If you want to rise above everyone else and have that reflected in your paycheck, it's up to you to go the extra mile and increase your value."

"Because we get paid by the problems we serve and the value we bring to the marketplace?" DeMarcus said.

"Correct. That's why it's up to you to learn how to do more and become more."

"What do you mean by that exactly?"

"Well, the average shelf life of a college degree is five years. [3]

Meaning the majority of everything you learned from college is outdated or will be soon. So it is your job to continue to develop yourself. To read books, audiobooks, listen to podcasts, etc., that sharpen and increase your skills. We have to continually study to show ourselves approved.

Again: it's your responsibility to become more valuable. THAT is the true meaning of education."

"'True meaning of education?'" DeMarcus asked, confused.

"Most people don't understand the real meaning of education. The word 'education' comes from the Latin word 'educo', which means 'to draw out' or 'lead out.' TRUE education DeMarcus is learning how to get out of you all that was placed in you. So a true education is lifelong and intentional. That's why the Bible says 'Buy the truth and sell it not.'

"So again the goal is to increase your value. Look at Joseph. He was a slave in Potiphar's house and a prisoner. Even then he learned how to lead up and lead laterally. He went the extra mile in everything he did and increased his influence with everyone around him. Oh! Almost forgot..." George pulled out his phone and started scrolling. "There's one important thing about going the extra mile. Attitude. Having a good attitude when doing it. There are people who go extra but have such a rotten attitude when they do it. With that attitude, they repel more than they attract. Read this."

DeMarcus took the phone and looked at the highlighted Scripture. He read, "'Servants, respectfully obey your earthly masters but always with an eye to obeying the real Master, Christ. Don't just do what you have to do to get by, but work heartily, as Christ's servants doing what God wants you to do. And work with a smile on your face, always keeping in mind that no matter who happens to be giving the orders, you're really serving God. Good work will get you good pay from the Master, regardless of whether you are slave or free.'[4] Where do you find this stuff?" He said as he handed George back the phone.

"I'm giving you my secret stash," he said with a chuckle. George looked at his watch then stood up. "Look, real promotion ultimately comes from God," he said. "You may not want to be at the bookstore, I get it. And you should be looking elsewhere. What I am saying is while you're there do your best, increase your value, go the extra mile, and solve problems. That will prepare you for the next level. But...I gotta go. Let's talk soon."

And just like that, he was gone.

Chapter 12 - Persistence

A few weeks had passed since DeMarcus last spoke with George; DeMarcus did indeed put the extra mile principle to work. He did more, looked for problems, and had a pleasing attitude. He worked like he was working for Christ Himself.

Everyone noticed the change. His supervisor told him to keep up the good work, and others were happy to see the "new" DeMarcus. Others were not. They felt that the better he did, the worse it made them look. DeMarcus was unfazed. He just found more ways to help and kept a good attitude even towards them. The more they were indifferent or unkind to him, the more he was kind and helpful to them.

Soon DeMarcus' influence had grown to the point that no major decision was done without his input. But his influence didn't affect his pay. He saw no signs of the house or any way of getting it. Every day he felt like quitting. What was really the point?

He was seriously contemplating giving up when he got a text from George. He wanted to meet later in the week. As grateful as he was for the meetup, this was the first time he didn't want to meet George. "Unless he got a bag of money for me," he thought.

He reluctantly agreed.

A few days passed and DeMarcus walked towards the cafe where he was going to meet George. He was even more frustrated. Nothing changed. There was no house. No extra money. No job that would use his strengths. He was still at the bookstore. Still in the apartment. And still no closer than when he started.

Or so he felt.

When he entered the cafe, he saw George seated sipping a cup of coffee. He was reading an article on his phone. He was so engrossed in the article he didn't acknowledge DeMarcus when he first sat down. A few seconds passed then George looked up, "How are you?"

"I'm good. Can't complain," DeMarcus said.

"Yes, you can. You choose not to," George responded.

"I guess you're right."

"But you do seem more down than usual. What's going on?"

"I'm good."

"Hmmm...you don't sound 'good.' Want to give up yet?"

"What?"

"You heard me. Do you want to give up yet?"

DeMarcus looked down for a second. He tried to keep his feelings bottled up. Then he looked up at George and everything spewed out. He spoke about his going the extra mile, the notoriety it was bringing, but none of that notoriety was affecting his paycheck, the frustration of not finding the house, and the equal frustration of not having the money. He spoke about his feeling of failure: of not being able to provide for his mom.

George listened patiently to his frustrations, his anxieties, and his doubts.

"And honestly I don't know what else to do," DeMarcus finished with a sigh.

"The only thing you can do right now is NOT quit," George started. "What you're experiencing is natural.

Especially when you don't see anything happening, but I can guarantee you this: it will NEVER happen if you give up. There were plenty of days when I was building MY career and nothing was going right. The only reason I'm here is that I decided to see this through. And you need patience, 'that, after you have done the will of God, you might receive the promise.' [1]

In fact, do you know why I modeled my career after John D. Rockefeller?"

"Cause he was rich?" DeMarcus said with a shrug.

"No. It was because of how he handled adversity. His mother was a single mom; his father was a womanizer. Meaning he had another family and was gone for long periods of time. So it came to a point that Rockefeller needed to get a job to help support the family. He was 16 years old. He looked for work for 6 weeks, 6 days a week. He left in the morning--usually, 8 am and came back late in the evening. What got me was that the average person might have been discouraged. Not Rockefeller. He grew more determined with each rejection. When I read that and saw his later success, I knew that quality I needed to have. And that is the quality you need to have DeMarcus."

DeMarcus thought about what George said. He was right. Nothing was going to happen if he just gave up.

"Another thing," George said, disturbing DeMarcus' train of thought. "Most believers are very weak in this respect. They expect God to just do it. And if He doesn't do it in 30 days or less, they completely fall off the belief train. They completely forget that perseverance is one of the fruits of the Spirit. [2]

They think that unless a blessing is instantaneous, it's not a blessing. Well, my business and career have been a blessing to many people, and it was NOT instantaneous. There were many times I wondered if we were going to make it, if I made the right decision, if I was in the right market, and etc. And there were MANY days I wanted to pack everything up and call it quits. That's why I didn't reach out to you these last few weeks."

"Wait, what?"

"You heard me. I wanted to see how you would handle the inevitable delay; because every breakthrough has a delay. And it's during this point you're faced with two options: quitting or persevering. Your mind is going to tell you to quit, and you're going to have to tell yourself to keep going. Have you ever heard of Folorunsho Alakija?"

"Doesn't ring a bell," DeMarcus said.

"She is a billionaire and Nigeria's richest woman. I never met her, but I followed her story. She began her entrepreneurial career as a fashion designer--then she and her family decided they wanted to get into oil exploration. When she ventured into that business, many doors were shut in her face. She kept knocking. When she applied for a license to get an oil bloc, her applications were put to the side. She kept applying. Then after 3 years, her application was approved. She got an oil bloc no one wanted. She found technical partners but after a while, they pulled out. So she and her husband used their life savings to secure the oil license. After 3 years they found new technical partners. Then after another 3 years, they struck oil in commercial quantities."

"I get it, I get it. Don't give up. Keep my eye on the prize," DeMarcus said.

"Can I finish?" George said, slightly annoyed.

DeMarcus didn't say another word.

"As I was saying," George started again. "When she struck oil, the unthinkable happened: the Nigerian government snatched a 40% stake. Then they later snatched an additional 10%."

DeMarcus kept his mouth shut. But he had a look of shock on his face.

"Because they were corrupt," George kept going unfazed. "They couldn't pass up the revenue from an 'unwanted' but now highly profitable oil bloc. So Alakija was devastated. She had two options: leave it alone like other companies who were victims of the government's greed OR fight back standing on constitutional rights. Do you know what most believers would've done?" George raised his hands and looked up to the sky. "'Well, it must not be God's Will.' 'If this was for me, it wouldn't be this hard.' 'God knows I tried.' 'The Lord giveth and the Lord taketh away.'" He lowered his hands.

"I see your point," DeMarcus said. "What did Alakija do?"

"She fought. She took the government to court. And she fought for 12 years. She fought when friends and advisers said there was no way she would win. She fought through sleepless nights. She fought through up and down battles. But in the end, she and her family won. Now, what were you saying about wanting to quit?"

DeMarcus just sat there. He felt like a fool. George said nothing, but he knew the point was made. These were things he wished he knew as a young man. He was happy to teach it. But he looked at his watch and realized he had to go. He reached into his pocket, grabbed his phone, did his familiar scroll, and handed the phone to DeMarcus. DeMarcus took the phone out of his hand and began to read. He read, "'Ask and keep on asking and it will be given to you; seek and keep on seeking and you will find; knock and keep on knocking and the door will be opened to you.'" [3]

George took the phone from DeMarcus' hand, stood up, put a hand on his shoulder, and said, "Keep going."

With that, he walked off.

Chapter 13 - Stewardship

Two months had passed since DeMarcus last met with George. DeMarcus' influence at the bookstore continued to skyrocket. He updated the bookstore's technology. He decreased inventory by tracking what consumers wanted and didn't want. He suggested having events showcasing up-and-coming Christian artists. He believed the budding community would increase sales.

He was right.

Word of his impact soon reached church leadership. The Bishop came to meet and personally thank him. Soon he was working on IT- related services for the church.

His mother was so proud.

Yet, none of this contributed significantly to his bottom line. He saw a pay increase but not enough to purchase his home. And even though he was narrowing his selections to Valley Stream or Lynbrook--two towns in Nassau his mother spoke favorably about-- he still didn't see a career.

But every time he was tempted to get discouraged, he'd encourage himself. "Focus on the mission, not your feelings," he said to himself. He continued his tithing (upping the percentage to 13%), his confessions, and kept the vision in front of him but still felt like he was missing something.

It was time to reach out to George.

George was going through changes himself. His company was preparing to go public. He spent his days meeting with underwriters, institutional investors, venture capitalists, etc. The company was also in the spotlight with all the media coverage. But the news outlets covered the CEO, not the CTO, so he was able to maintain a degree of anonymity.

DeMarcus texted George and George suggested they meet at his office for lunch.

Two days later, DeMarcus made the familiar trek to George's office. He was ushered in and saw George at his desk finishing up a call. He sat in front of George's desk and surveyed the office while waiting for George to finish.

He could hear George finishing the call and turned around to face him. He said his goodbyes and looked at DeMarcus.

"Well aren't you busy," DeMarcus said.

"More than you realize. It is extremely time-consuming and expensive to go public. Not very fun to be honest. But it'll be over soon."

"So...does that mean you'll be a billionaire soon?" DeMarcus asked.

"What it means is that I'll be retired soon. After this is over, I'll be turning over the reins to new leadership," George said.

"So what's next?"

"Whatever God has for me. But enough about me, what's going on with you?" George asked.

DeMarcus shared with George everything that took place with the bookstore, the Bishop, the house, and even his mom's admiration. He told him that he forced himself to keep going every time he was tempted to quit. "But," DeMarcus said. "I still haven't found a career and the money for this house."

“You’re on your way,” George said assuredly. “What you’ve done is increase your value. And there’s no way a person of value stays unnoticed. The Bible says, ‘Seest thou a man diligent in his business? he shall stand before kings; he shall not stand before mean men.’ [1]

‘Mean men’ means ordinary people. Joseph was in prison and his name still reached Pharaoh. You just keep doing what you’re doing. Let’s go get some food.”

They walked to the cafeteria downstairs. On the way, George spoke to many other employees who either simply greeted him or asked his advice on a project. DeMarcus was fascinated by how admired and loved he was. He wasn’t seen as a boss, he was a leader. “Help me Lord to be the kind of leader He is,” DeMarcus silently prayed.

They got to the cafeteria, ordered their food, and went back to George’s office. Once there, DeMarcus stated his primary concern: “I feel like I’m missing something. I’m doing everything you’re telling me to do and I still don’t see the money.”

George picked at his salad and let the comment hang in the air. “Well, you still do need patience...but you’re right. There is something you are missing. The next step is for you to learn how to be a better steward. A better steward of money.”

“But aren’t I tithing? Isn’t that enough?” DeMarcus asked, surprised.

“Tithing and giving are part of it, not all of it,” George said. “Let’s first define what a steward is. A steward is someone entrusted to manage resources - particularly money. A Biblical steward has to be two things: faithful and profitable. Do you remember that story where Jesus multiplied the fish and the loaves? Do you know what He did next? He ordered the disciples to pick up the fragments. [2] Why? Simple. He hates waste. So if Jesus hates waste, it's safe to say that God hates waste. Right?"

"Makes sense," DeMarcus said, nodding.

"And if God hates waste," George started. "Why would he give a lot to someone who can only handle a little? That would create waste right there."

"Are you saying I can only handle a little?" DeMarcus asked defensively.

"I'm saying that we are rarely trained on how to manage money. Make it yes. Manage and multiply it no. I learned how to manage money on a small scale so now I can manage it on a much bigger scale. But that was because I became financially literate on both a psychological level and a practical level."

"What do you mean 'psychological?'"

"Well...we all have a money blueprint. It's based on how we were raised. For instance, you could have people growing up hearing this around the dinner table: 'money doesn't grow on trees' or 'what do I look like...Rockefeller' or 'money is evil' or 'those rich people are bad.' What these people will then do is subconsciously sabotage their own success. They'll find ways to get rid of money, not manage it properly, etc. Why? They're fulfilling their blueprint. There are a lot of people who want to be 'successful' but keep finding ways to sabotage themselves. That's why the first thing we did was work on renewing your mind. None of this would've worked with a poverty mindset."

"Ok. Mind blown," DeMarcus said with a chuckle.

"In fact," George said. "I know a couple who always had money fights. He was a saver, she was a spender. One night we had dinner and they were explaining their dilemma. I asked them both, 'how did your family talk about money?' The husband said that his family struggled a lot with money and he kept hearing his mom talk about how she didn't feel safe. So from there, he equated having a lot of money with safety and he felt 'unsafe' letting it go. Her upbringing was different. They were the upper-middle class and did many things that required money: vacations, eating out, etc. So she equated money as a tool used to enjoy life. So no wonder they couldn't see eye to eye."

"So who was right and who was wrong?"

"They both were right. They needed to be saving AND they needed to be enjoying life. But they both were wrong for not trying to understand the other person's blueprint. But I don't want to go too much into that. What I am saying to you DeMarcus, is that I don't want you to be a slave to a job. You should always be increasing your value, increasing your net worth, and increasing the number of income streams that come into your life."

"So wait," DeMarcus asked, confused. "You want me to have more than one job?"

"No. Absolutely not," George said. "I want you to get out of the mindset of trading time for money. Because you can have multiple income streams without having multiple jobs. I want you to cultivate the skill of getting money to work for you. When done right, money will always work harder than we ever can. In fact, when Jesus spoke about the parable of the talents, one translation said, 'The servant who had received five talents went and put them to work, and gained five more.'[3]

For instance, we have multiple income streams in our business. And outside of my company, I have other streams of income. Some real estate, some dividend-paying stocks, and some other smaller ventures. The point is: I don't believe in one stream of income and neither should you."

"I get that. But that's easy for you to say. You have a company which is probably worth billions. I don't have that," DeMarcus said.

"What you don't have right now is financial literacy," George said. "Not yet at least. It doesn't matter how much you make, it matters what you do with what you make. What you need to do now is to learn how money works. From there, you'll learn how to make it work for you."

DeMarcus thought about that. The concept of making money work for him seemed to be so out of reach. Yet it made sense. If he could discover how to make his money work for him, would he really have money problems?

"This concept might seem foreign," George continued. "It's not something preached from the pulpit, or taught in schools, or discussed in most homes. But I love the freedom of knowing that money is working for me. And because of my literacy, it'd be working for me whether I have my own company or not."

George looked at his watch. "I'm sorry, DeMarcus, we're going to have to cut this short. I have a meeting shortly. But...your assignment...should you choose to accept it..."

"So a little Mission Impossible humor, huh?" DeMarcus said jokingly

"You got it. But seriously, study to show yourself approved. Start reading magazines on finance. Start watching financial shows. Even if it makes absolutely no sense in the beginning. Keep doing it. Get some books on finance and invest in your education. It will pay dividends. I'll talk to you later."

With that, George whipped around to his computer and started typing. DeMarcus took that as his cue to leave.

Chapter 14 - Endgame

A full year passed since DeMarcus and George last met and a lot of things changed. George took his company public and effectively retired as CTO. For the first few months, he and his family traveled abroad. His wife and kids were excited for the free time and he was excited to give it to them.

On the other hand, DeMarcus continued to go the extra mile, while increasing his value and financial acumen. One day George reached out, saying they should catch up. DeMarcus agreed. They set a time for Saturday at the diner near Central Park. When the day came, DeMarcus got there ten minutes early to wait for his mentor. George walked in two minutes after the appointed time.

"You're late," DeMarcus said, looking at an imaginary watch.

"Oh! Well please forgive the disrespect sir," George said with a slight chuckle.

DeMarcus stood up and greeted George with a hug. They sat down, caught up for a few minutes, looked at the menu, ordered, and caught up again.

"So public company huh?" DeMarcus started. "How does it feel?"

"It feels like something I don't want to do again, to be honest," he said. "But if I do it will be behind the scenes as an investor."

"What have you been doing since you stepped down?"

"Honestly," George started. "Taking the time to breathe. My personality is always to look for the next goal, opportunity, and conquest. But this time, I wanted to reflect on where I came from, what was accomplished, and what God did through me. Just for a little bit, I wanted to be still and know that He is God." [1]

"Hmmmmm...I hear that."

"Also been traveling with the family." George continued. "The Lord reminded me that I wasn't the only one who did this--they did it with me. My wife sacrificed a lot as did my kids. So they needed a reprieve too. But enough about me, how have you been doing Mr. Superstar?"

"Well...a lot has changed." DeMarcus started. "I now work full time as an IT technician."

"Wow. Good for you. You sent out a lot of resumes?" George asked.

"Not quite. I was still doing my thing at the bookstore and the Bishop gave me more work to do at the church. Apparently, he was talking about me and the great work I was doing in a leadership meeting. One of the deacons was a Director at my new company. Long story short, they offered me a job at nearly triple the salary of the bookstore. I still do some part-time work for the church and bookstore, but the position is a better fit, and they're talking about moving me into a managerial role. Considering the fact that I've only been there a couple of months, it has to be nothing but the grace of God."

"I agree. Faith works when you work it," George said. "So since you're making all this money, you're just saving up for the house I assume?"

"Not quite."

George gave him a quizzical look.

“I decided to invest in rental property, and I’m holding it in an LLC,” he continued. “Keeps my personal stuff protected and lets me run it like a real business.”

“Hmmm...why the rental property?” George asked.

“I was doing research and I thought if I just buy the home I'll be paying for the home. But if I buy rental property...”

“...the other homes will pay for your home.” George finished.

“Right! And the tax side is what got me. Between the depreciation write-offs, deducting the expenses, and being able to roll the gains from one property into the next without getting taxed, the numbers just work. I did a LOT of due diligence on it and it made the most sense.”

George sat there admiring his student. Not only had he become a man of God, but he also became a man of the market. There was no telling how far he could go. At that moment, the waitress came with their orders. They thanked her, prayed over their food, and started to eat.

“So how does mom feel about all of this?” George asked.

“Well, she doesn’t know that I am doing this to get her house. But she is happy with the career change...and my overall growth. Speaking of which...” DeMarcus took his phone out of his pocket, scrolled through some verses, and handed the phone to George. “Here, read this.”

George smiled as he took the phone. “Yes sir. ‘And they that shall be of thee shall build the old waste places: thou shalt raise up the foundations of many generations; and thou shalt be called, The repairer of the breach, The restorer of paths to dwell in.’[2] Ok?”

"So I was reading one day and that Scripture jumped out at me. I couldn't shake it so I prayed about it for a few days. I felt like God was showing me my purpose and it had to do with mentorship."

"What do you mean?" George asked as he put down his fork.

"Well...our time together was really life-changing. For a long time, I was blaming God for 'taking' my dad. It took me a while to realize that He didn't take him from me. And the truth is, I'll probably never know the reason until I get to heaven. But him not being here left a real void. I was struggling with this thing called manhood and I didn't even know it. You really helped me to cross that bridge. And even though I'm not 'there' I'm not where I was. Thank you..."

His voice trailed off. The moment was filled with emotion. DeMarcus looked down at his food while George looked to his right. No eye contact. It took a while for both men to gather themselves. DeMarcus started again.

"It got me thinking: 'how many other young men need this? How many other men don't know what you taught me? And I'm not even talking about kids in the street...I'm talking about other young men in the church."

"So what are you saying?"

"I think using what you taught me as a base, I want to mentor other young men."

George thought for a second. "Well, there definitely is a void and a need. And I never really thought of the fact that there is a generation of young men who need mentorship. That is an awesome idea, DeMarcus! How are you going to get started?"

"I spoke to the Bishop about it. He loves it. He just doesn't feel that I'm ready to do it on my own. He thinks it would make more sense to partner with someone more..." he paused as he looked for the appropriate word. "Seasoned."

"'Seasoned,' eh?" George asked with a slight smile.

"Well...I think it would make sense. Don't you?"

George thought for a while. "I'll have to pray on it and talk to my wife, but unless she and God have an objection...I think it might make sense."

They sat there the rest of the lunch talking, strategizing, and searching Scripture. A few months later, they began their first "Band of Brothers" meetup. It started small, but word spread and it continued to grow.

Meanwhile, DeMarcus continued to grow in his spiritual and professional walk. He continued his ascent up the ranks becoming the fastest and youngest vice president in company history. He continued to buy rental property, invested wisely, and soon bought the family home in cash.

With his promotion and other streams of income, he effectively retired his mom. She didn't have to worry about another bill. Delores herself could hardly believe what Dad had done for her in a few short years. She praised Him for her son, her home, and new ability to travel more. She'd often say, "Weeping may endure for a night but joy comes in the morning. Thank You Daddy for the morning!"

George also continued his mentorship of DeMarcus and other young men. Professionally he never did take an active role in corporate leadership but became a venture capitalist to other young startups.

References

Chapter 1 - Wretched Man

[1] Romans 7:23-25 (TLB)

Chapter 2 - Backdrop

[1] Song of Solomon 3:1-4 (KJV)

[2] Matthew 11:28-29 (KJV)

[3] Revelation 22:16

[4] Revelation 1:8

[5] "The Lily of the Valley" a gospel hymn, It was written by Charles W. Fry in 1881.

[6] Romans 2:4 (KJV)

[7] Proverbs 17:6 (BSB)

Chapter 4 - Confrontation

[1] James 1:27 (KJV)

Chapter 5 - The Great Confession

[1] Jeremiah 1:12

[2] John 15:5 (NIV)

[3] Job 31:1 (NIV)

[4] 1 Thessalonians 4:3-4 (KJV)

[5] 1 Thessalonians 4:6-8 (NIV)

[6] I would recommend "God's Creative Power for Finances" by Charles & Annette Capps.

Chapter 6 - Generosity

[1] Joshua 1:8

[2] Taanit 9a

[3] Proverbs 11:24 (NKJV)

[4] R.G. Le Tourneau--Mover of Men and Mountains pg 193

[5] 2 Corinthians 9:6-11 (AMPC)

[6] John 6:1-14

[7] Jeremiah 29:11 (NIV)

[8] Luke 6:38 (KJV)

Chapter 7 - Making the Cut

[1] Philippians 4:19 (NKJV)
[2] Psalms 36:8
[3] Matthew 6:25-34 (NKJV)
[4] Philippians 3:13-14 (KJV)

Chapter 8 - Purpose

[1] Ephesians 1:11-12 MSG
[2] Ecclesiastes 1:2 (ESV)
[3] 2 Corinthians 10:13-16 (NKJV)
[4] Isaiah 32:8 (Bible in Basic English)
[5] Giving It All Away...and Getting It All Back Again: The Way of Living Generously, location 950, Kindle Edition
[6] Isaiah 55:8-9
[7] 1 Corinthians 1:27

Chapter 9 - Vision

[1] Ecclesiastes 5:3 (KJV)
[2] Numbers 13:32-33 (NKJV)
[3] Philippians 4:13 (NKJV)
[4] 1 John 3:2 (MSG)
[5] Habakkuk 2:2
[6] Proverbs 4:26-27 (MSG)
[7] Proverbs 24:27 (TLB)
[8] 2 Corinthians 1:20

Chapter 10 - Underwriting

[1] Psalms 46:1 (KJV)
[2] 1 Peter 2:21 (KJV)
[3] Proverbs 11:14

Chapter 11 - The Extra Mile

[1] Matthew 5:41 (NKJV)
[2] Mark 15:21-22
[3] "Mind the Skills Gap." Harvard Business Review. https://hbr.org/2012/09/mind-the-skills-gap
[4] Ephesians 6:5-8 (MSG)

Chapter 12 - Persistence

[1] Hebrews 10:36 (KJV)
[2] Galatians 5:22-23
[3] Matthew 7:7 (AMPC)

Chapter 13 - Stewardship

[1] Proverbs 22:29 (KJV)
[2] John 6:12
[3] Matthew 25:16 (Berean Study Bible)

Chapter 14 - Endgame

[1] Psalms 46:10
[2] Isaiah 58:12 (KJV)

Discussion Guide

Group Reading Guide

This guide is built for groups reading together — in a small group, a mentorship circle, or a band of brothers like the one DeMarcus and George start at the end of the book. Work through it a section at a time, or in one sitting. There are no wrong answers, only honest ones. Bring a Bible. Be willing to be the man in the room who answers first.

Getting Started

1. DeMarcus begins the book living a "double life" — church on the outside, a private struggle underneath. Where do you most feel the gap between who you are in public and who you are in private?
2. Delores prays for "a MAN who could reach" her son, because she knows she cannot raise a man by herself. Who were the men who reached you? Who is reaching for you now?
3. George is the richest man in the church, and almost no one knows it. Why do you think he keeps it hidden? What does that say about how he sees his wealth?

The Wretched Man — Identity Before Behavior

4. George tells DeMarcus that the most effective way to change your life is from identity, not from actions — "I'm not a smoker" versus "I'm trying to quit." Where in your own life have you been fighting a behavior without first settling an identity?

5. DeMarcus saw himself as "trying to be right," not as "righteous." How would your week look different if you truly believed you already were who God says you are?
6. George calls Scripture "Script-ure" — the programming we speak over ourselves. What "scripts" did you inherit growing up, about yourself, money, or God? Which ones need to be rewritten?

Generosity and Stewardship — Money as a Tool

7. George says a biblical steward must be two things: faithful and profitable. Which of those two do you find harder, and why?
8. The book describes a "money blueprint" formed by what we heard around the dinner table growing up. What did your family teach you about money — in words, and in actions?
9. DeMarcus struggles with the idea of giving away the very thing he needs. Have you ever experienced giving leading to increase — financial or otherwise? What held you back when you didn't give?
10. George distinguishes the tithe (what we return) from the offering (what we freely give). What would generosity "above the tithe" look like in your life this year?

Purpose and Vision — Knowing Whose You Are

11. George draws an arrow: Purpose leads to Vision, and Vision serves the original Purpose. In one sentence, what do you believe your purpose is? If you don't know yet, what's one thing you could start doing to find out?

12. The men in the jungle make great progress — in the wrong jungle. Where might you be working hard at something that isn't actually yours to do?
13. DeMarcus writes ten goals, then circles one: buy his mother a house. What is the one goal that, if you accomplished it, would change not just your life but the lives of people you love?
14. George asks whether DeMarcus is "interested" in his goal or "committed" to it — the difference being what you'll do when it's not convenient. Name a goal you've been merely interested in. What would commitment require?

The Extra Mile and Persistence — Doing the Work

15. Going the extra mile made DeMarcus indispensable, but it didn't change his paycheck right away. Have you ever done the right thing for a long time before seeing any reward? How did you keep going?
16. George deliberately goes silent for weeks to see whether DeMarcus will quit in the delay. Why do you think "the delay" is where most people give up? Where are you in a delay right now?
17. Folorunsho Alakija fought for twelve years to keep what was hers. What is something in your life worth fighting that long for?

Mentorship, Fatherhood, and the Wound

18. The hardest thing DeMarcus carries is the belief that God "killed" his father. Have you carried a wound you

blamed on God? What did honesty about that wound make possible — or what might it make possible now?

19. George says he is not trying to "raise" DeMarcus, only to "help" him. Why does that distinction matter? What's the difference between a mentor and a father, and where do the two overlap?
20. By the end, DeMarcus wants to mentor other young men in the church the same way he was mentored. Who is the one younger man you could pour into right now? What's stopping you from starting?
21. George never sought the spotlight, yet his quiet life changed everything for one young man. What would it look like for your influence to be "felt by all" without being seen by all?

Going Further — This Week

22. Write down ten goals for the next five years, the way George had DeMarcus do. Circle the one that matters most. Put it where you'll see it every day.
23. Find and write down ten Scriptures related to an area where you need breakthrough — finances, freedom, family, purpose. Speak them, morning and evening, for the next thirty days.
24. Identify one mentor you want to learn from (living or not, met or unmet) and one younger man you could mentor. Take one concrete step toward each this week.
25. Decide on one act of generosity "above the tithe" and do it before the group meets again.

www.ingramcontent.com/pod-product-compliance
Ingram Content Group UK Ltd.
Pitfield, Milton Keynes, MK11 3LW, UK
UKHW041829200726
13854UKWH00002BA/904